Christian Prayer
and Healing

By the same author:

Love that heals

Christian Prayer and Healing

Andy Arbuthnot

HIGHLAND BOOKS

ISBN: 0 946616 59 0

Cover design: Diane Drummond

Quotations from the Bible are from the New
International Version, unless otherwise stated.

Royalties from this book will be donated to the
London Healing Mission

The talks on which this book is based were recorded
by Anchor Recordings, 72 The Street, Kennington,
Ashford, Kent TN24 9HS.

Printed in Great Britain for
HIGHLAND BOOKS
Broadway House, The Broadway
Crowborough, East Sussex TN6 1BY
by Richard Clay Ltd, Bungay, Suffolk.
Typeset by Rowland Phototypesetting Ltd,
Bury St Edmunds, Suffolk

To Audrey,

My wife and my partner in the healing ministry, without whose constant love, support and encouragement, none of this would have happened.

CONTENTS

INTRODUCTION

Every month we have a regular teaching day here at the London Healing Mission. This book has grown out of those teaching days.

The original purpose was to share some of the insights which the Lord in His mercy and His kindness had shown us. We wanted to help those who came, so that they themselves might pray more effectively and with more power, and that all might be done to the glory of God and the spreading of His Kingdom.

Subsequently we realised, from the many lovely letters we received, that through the teaching days the people who came had themselves grown into a deeper knowledge of the Lord, and a more wonderful awareness of His presence. For this we thank God.

We always remember that when St Paul lists the gifts of the Holy Spirit (1 Cor 12.9), his reference to 'healing' is in the plural – 'the gifts of healing'. There may well be others to whom the Lord has given different gifts of healing. If so, our purpose is not to say, 'You've got it wrong', but simply to pass on what we have learnt here, and how we have seen God working in our midst.

Paul wrote to the church in Corinth, 'The Kingdom of God is not a matter of talk but of power' (1 Cor 4.20). Jesus' own ministry was essentially a ministry of power. The ministry of the early church was a ministry of power. Until the power to set people free, to give them His inner peace and to make them whole, comes back into His body, the Church, it will continue to seem irrelevant in the lives of most people.

My grateful thanks go to Jacqui Dowdy, who has typed and retyped the manuscript with unfailing cheerfulness – even when her home was broken into and her word processor was stolen, together with the book!

Andy Arbuthnot
The London Healing Mission
20 Dawson Place
London W2 4TL

1

'Reveal Me to Them'

This was crisis.

It seemed that all my training for the past three years had been leading up to this point. Yet I was completely unprepared. I did not know what to do.

That was in the early spring of 1975. I was approaching fifty and my secular career was getting more and more demanding; that was indeed part of the trouble. A year before, I had taken over as Chairman and Chief Executive of one of the older merchant banking groups in the City of London, Arbuthnot Latham. In financial terms, we were small compared to our competitors, but we had a broadly-based business and employed about a thousand people. Competition, as always in the City of London, was intense.

My role as the one responsible for our group, involved much hard work and too much time, but the problem I was facing that day, early in 1975, didn't arise from my City work. Some years previously, I had felt that the Lord was calling me into the ordained ministry in the Church of England. I had been ordained some six months earlier and it had seemed right to join

what the Church of England calls the non-stipendiary
ministry. That meant that I continued with my job in
the City and only put on a dog-collar for one evening
and at weekends.

When my friends complained sometimes about the
pressures upon those in positions of responsibility in the
City, I used to suggest their becoming clergymen; I
knew of few better ways of putting business problems
out of one's mind than waking up on a Saturday
morning and knowing that one had to make sense for
some twenty minutes or so in the pulpit the following
day!

Sixteen of us had been on a three-year course which
was specifically designed for training those who were
already in full-time employment. It was the same
training for all of us, regardless of whether we were
going on to stipendiary ministry, working full-time in
the Church, or, as I did, to the non-stipendiary ministry. But the course had not taught us what would be
involved in taking a children's service on Good Friday.

The problem which confronted me that evening in
the early spring of 1975 was that I was due to take the
children's service on the morning of Good Friday. I had
not been to a children's service for forty years. My vicar
was ill, so I couldn't consult him, and, because of
pressures in the City, I had virtually no time to prepare
the service.

This would be the first time that I was to take a
service on my own, and it seemed that all the training of
the previous three years had led up to this point. Yet I
had no idea what to do. How did one arrange the
service? What reading should I have? What hymns
should I choose? What prayers? And, above all, what
should I preach about?

At the time my wife, Audrey, and I had the use of one of the curate's houses in the parish of Mortlake, and I went up to our bedroom with the problem in the forefront of my mind. I started to pray. What else could I do? I cried out: 'Lord, I don't want to let You down. Lord, I don't know what to do and I've no-one to ask. Lord, tell me what to do!'

'Reveal Me to them.'

The answer came back instantaneously and clearly, in a man's voice. My first reaction was one of terror. There was someone in the room with me whom I couldn't see, but who was intelligent, someone who had heard my prayer and who had given me an immediate answer. Later, I came to understand very well why, when an angel or a messenger appeared to men in biblical times, his first words so often were, 'Fear not'. I knew that I was experiencing the same immediate reaction of fear as, for instance, Mary had felt when the angel Gabriel appeared to her (Lk 1.29), or the shepherds had experienced when the angel announced to them the birth of Jesus (Lk 2.9).

But the fear lasted only for an instant. Then the Lord spoke to me in the way He usually does speak to us, and some words just popped into my mind. This time the words, unspoken, were from Jesus' conversation with the woman at the well in John's Gospel. They were, 'God is Spirit' (Jn 4.24).

I just burst out laughing. As I remembered those words, I realised that this was God Himself who had spoken to me. The fear had vanished and the laughter expressed, on the one hand, my relief, and on the other, a great feeling of joy.

I don't remember the details of that service but I do remember that it went well. How could it have done otherwise with that direct leading from the Lord Himself? As Audrey and I were walking back from the church a woman stopped as she cycled past. 'My friend has just told me what a wonderful service she had with you in Christ Church', she said. 'I thought I must stop and tell you.'

Often in the Bible there is a double meaning when the Lord speaks. Often His words convey His solution to the problem of the moment, but also His words give ongoing guidance and instruction. It was a while before I came to realise that the words I had heard were not just an expression of what the Lord in His mercy wanted me to do that Good Friday morning. They were also His ongoing instructions to me, not only for every sermon I should ever preach, but, as I came to see it later still, for the whole of the rest of my life.

Since then I have, not unnaturally, taken a keen interest when people have shared with me that they have heard the Lord speaking to them in an audible voice. I think I have met some six or seven people who have had this same experience – although, interestingly, I have never met anyone who has heard the Lord speaking audibly to them twice. I know, for my part, there have been times since that Good Friday when I have earnestly asked the Lord to answer me in a clear voice as He did on that occasion. But He has not done it a second time.

Among those I have met who have heard Him speak I remember a woman in her middle thirties who told me that some ten years earlier, she had been, as she put it, 'between boyfriends'. A young man had asked if he could take her out in his car, and, having no boyfriend for the moment, she accepted. She told me that he wasn't her type at all, and one can imagine her amazement as they were driving along in the car, when she heard an audible voice saying to her, 'I want you to marry this man.'

Then there was the young man in his late twenties who told me that one evening as he was running his bath the Holy Spirit fell powerfully upon him. He turned off the taps and sank to his knees at the edge of the bath – there was nothing else he could do. He was baptised in the Holy Spirit and he too heard a clear and audible voice. It told him that God wanted him to marry a certain girl.

He had never even taken the girl out. He told me how curious it felt taking a girl out for the first time, and going through all the stages of getting to know her and falling in love with her when, from the beginning, he knew that she was going to be his wife. When I met them they seemed remarkably happy.

When I was a little boy I remember my mother reading me an Old Testament story. I asked her, 'Mum, how does God speak to people?' She said she thought He spoke out of a cloud or something in Old Testament times – but, of course, He didn't do it now. My mother died but how surprised she would have been – and how delighted – if she had known that one day the Lord was going to give a clear and audible instruction to her son.

2

On Putting the Lord First

'God must have common sense', we kept saying to ourselves. As 1982 drew to a close, it was becoming increasingly clear that after eight years of ministry the Lord was telling us to go to the London Healing Mission. When we prayed He seemed to be saying that, and Christian friends whom we consulted confirmed it. The problem was that we knew next to nothing about the Christian healing ministry.

Eventually I wrote to the trustees of the Healing Mission saying that we felt the Lord might be leading us to take over. I added that very likely we were hearing wrongly, but perhaps they would let me come and pray with them that the Lord might guide them in the choice of the next missioner.

They invited me to attend the next trustees' meeting. I would gladly have fallen through the floor when I entered the room and heard the senior trustee introducing me with the words, 'This is the man God has chosen to head the London Healing Mission!' Thus we were appointed to take over at the mission – despite the fact that a couple of years earlier Audrey was on record as saying, 'The London Healing Mission? It's the last place on earth I'd ever go to.'

But the difficulty was that we didn't know what to do. However, we looked at each other and said, 'God must have common sense. If He has put us here to run the Healing Mission He must realise that we don't know what to do. All we need to do is wait on Him and listen to what He says.'

It was amazing how the Lord led us. But then if one trusts Him, and seeks wholeheartedly to do His will, He does guide us. Nonetheless, we were both extremely surprised to receive a letter from a firm of Christian book publishers when we had been here for less than a year, asking us to write a book about our work. I rang to say, 'I think your secretary must have made a mistake. I imagine you want a short article.' I nearly fell off my chair at the answer, 'No, we want a book, if you would write one for us.' The book was entitled *Love that Heals*.

In our work, we counsel people and we pray with them, but this present book is not primarily about counselling. Many good books have been written on the subject. Much excellent work is done by Christians who are engaged in counselling. But in the work to which the Lord has called us counselling forms only one part. This book is about praying with power.

Part of the reason for this is that people often travel a long way to us. I used to say that people came from all over the south of England, but Audrey pointed out that people have come from all over the country, and indeed some have come for ministry from overseas.

They may be with us for only an hour-and-a-half, and we have to minister the healing and wholeness of the Lord to them in that time. Under those circumstances a prolonged course of counselling is not possible. We have to pray for them in power.

In our earlier book, we told how E had come, having suffered for many years from depression. Each time she came she was accompanied by her friend, J, who is a lovely Christian woman in her late forties. The last time they came together I asked E what we were going to pray for. 'I'm fine!' she replied with the broadest of smiles. It was clear that the Lord had healed her. For the rest of the time she and I ministered together to her friend J.

Some months later, J came to see me herself, this time alone. 'You must understand,' she said, 'that for the last two years I've been going to –' and she mentioned a well-known counselling centre in London, – 'and they've helped me a lot. They're good people,' she stressed. 'But,' she continued, 'I've come here today because I want to be healed.' Clearly, no more talking was necessary so we got straight down to prayer. The Lord healed her that afternoon.

The Lord can use both the skill of the trained counsellor and the humility of the one who prays, to lead a person towards the wholeness He longs for in each of us.

Many people feel, perhaps unconsciously, that they must reach a certain standard of holiness before they can pray in power. This is not true. I read about a vicar who led his somewhat unwilling team into having regular healing services. He recounted how the first miracle came at the hands of a curate who up to then had been thoroughly sceptical about this whole healing business.

A woman discussed with me whether it would be right for her to come to one of our teaching days. I knew that there was still a lot of healing that the Lord longed to do in her, and she knew it too. 'But people keep coming to me and somehow I seem able to help them,' she said. We welcomed her to our next teaching day. If the Lord waited until we were perfect before He could use us, all ministry would come to a rapid halt.

At the same time, if we feel that the Lord is leading us to pray for other people, we need to bear in mind the words in James' letter, 'If anyone is sick, let him send for the elders of the church' (Jas 5.14 AV). Normally it is right for them to seek help themselves. Then we go to them with joyful hearts, confident that the Lord will respond. However much we may feel we are called to pray for the sick, it is normally wrong for us to go round offering to pray with people.

It is the Lord's ministry. Our role is simply to love Him and make ourselves available to Him so that His power may flow into us and may flow through us to fulfil His wonderful purpose. Often as I minister I hear myself praying, 'Lord, forgive me for being here. Lord, You love this person. You long to help them and make them whole. Lord, please just release Your wonderful healing power on them and don't pay any attention to me'.

A few days ago I had a letter from a vicar in Sunderland. Two of his parishioners had evidently been much helped when they came to see one of the team here. The vicar described how the Holy Spirit was moving in power in his church. 'I'm not sure whether I'm just an onlooker,' he wrote, 'or whether I'm actually being used.'

When I was ordained and still working in the City of London I can remember for several months praying with much agitation, 'Lord, there are so few of us in this great heathen city. How am I going to set about converting them?' It seemed that the reply He gave me in prayer was, 'It is my role to speak to my people in their hearts. You just do what you're told to do.' That reply freed me from worrying. All we need to do is to move quietly on, following where He leads, and praying for people. Then we leave Him to work in power to His glory.

Every now and then, someone comes saying, 'I feel I'm running out of steam. I keep trying to do what I believe the Lord has called me to do, but it's becoming more and more of an effort. I no longer feel close to Him.' When they first became Christians there was such a lovely sense of intimacy with the Lord. They felt Jesus was close to them as they prayed – and now it all seemed to have gone.

'Do you realise,' we often ask, 'that there is one thing in life more important than doing God's work?' A question like that can bring a conversation to a sudden halt. What could be more important than doing God's work? The answer is, of course, that God Himself is more important than His work. Jesus told us that the most important thing is to love God, God who revealed Himself in Jesus (Mk 12.30).

Jesus added that the second of the two great commandments was for us to love our neighbour as ourself (Mk 12.31). This second commandment comprises all that we do in prayer for other people, in helping them, and in serving them.

Many people, perhaps unconsciously, say to themselves, 'Well, I don't really understand how to love God and I know I'm not very good at it, so I'm going to settle for the second great commandment. No doubt, sometime in the future, I will find out how to love God and then I'll start putting that commandment first.'

If we thus invert the two great commandments, we are disobeying Jesus. Before long we will lose our sense of intimacy with Him and, in our work for those around us, we will run dry.

Two thousand years ago, when Jesus was on this earth, advanced thinkers in Jerusalem were puzzling over their situation. They had the law of Moses which we find in the earlier books of the Bible, and their predecessors had built up a mass of rules and regulations covering every activity in daily life. It simply wasn't possible, however, for them to observe all these regulations. 'There must be a key commandment underlying all these rules,' they reasoned. 'What is it?' they asked each other.

On several occasions they asked Jesus what in His view was the most important commandment. He probably had the question put to Him dozens of times. He replied that the law of Moses and all the rules and regulations were summed up in the two great commandments and quoted from the books of Deuteronomy and Leviticus. 'Love the Lord your God with all your heart and with all your soul, with all your mind. This is the first and greatest commandment. And . . . love your neighbour as yourself' (Mt 22.37,38).

I am sure there were those in religious circles in Jerusalem, of high intelligence, who prided themselves on their intellectual ability, on their own wisdom and understanding, who tended to dismiss Jesus' answer as being too simplistic as men do today.

But ever since mankind began to be civilised, the vast majority of men and women have been at best illiterate peasants, scratching their living from the soil by the sweat of their brow. Some have been uneducated slaves owned as chattels. Unless the Gospel of Jesus is sufficiently simple for all men and women to be able to understand it, then Christianity is of no use. Jesus Himself said, 'Unless you become like little children, you will never enter the kingdom of heaven' (Mt 18.3). A religion which requires a degree in theology is of no use to most of us, still less to a child.

Although God will always be a mystery and beyond the wisdom of the keenest intellect, Christ's basic message is simple: 'Love God, who revealed Himself in Jesus, with everything you've got and make Him absolutely central in your life.'

It is no use bothering about whatever ministry we think He has given us, it is no use even concerning ourselves with loving our neighbours as ourselves, unless we put this before anything else.

David Watson was probably the greatest Christian evangelist we have seen in this country since the war. His ministry was both national and international. Yet he died of cancer of the liver when he was fifty and despite the fact that countless Christians were praying fervently for his healing.

Why did God take him? We find the answer in David's last book *Fear no Evil*. He recounts how he kept praying, 'Lord, You have given me this remarkable ministry. Lord, I'm still quite young. Lord, You only have to reach out your finger and touch my liver and I shall be healed. Lord, do please make haste and heal me, as I want to get on with the ministry You've given me.'

David Watson wrote down the answer which the Lord gave him in prayer: 'David, I do understand about your ministry, but I want you to understand that my relationship of love with you is even more important.'

For twenty-five years, Jim Glennon ran the healing services in St Andrew's Cathedral, Sydney. Every Wednesday evening between five and six hundred people came to those healing services.

Jim recounts how as a young man, he prayed, 'Lord, what do You want me to do with my life?' Anyone could be forgiven who guessed that in His reply God would have revealed something of the healing ministry with which He was to endow Jim. But this was not the case. God didn't even reply, 'Jim, I want you to be a man of prayer.' The reply which Jim felt he had from the Lord was, 'I want you to learn to pray.' All that tremendous ministry of healing was simply a by-product. God was saying to Jim that He wanted him to put his relationship with God first. He wanted Jim to make himself available in prayer and He, the Lord, would then release to him the ministry which in His sovereign glory He would choose for him.

I found the same lesson in a book written by Pastor Yonggi Cho, minister of a church of nearly half a million people in Seoul, South Korea. (The church seats over 30,000 people. There are seven services every Sunday, and extensive use is made of overflow halls). He wrote that if at any time he felt the inner nudge of the Holy Spirit to go and pray, he would drop what he was doing and obey.

My first reaction when I read that was one of horror. Here was a man with a tremendous ministry, responsible for nearly half a million souls. Surely he needed to give every waking minute to the work to which the Lord had called him. Wasn't it irresponsible of him to break off in the middle of a busy day to go and pray?

Then it was as if a small voice said to me, 'Do *you* pastor a church of half a million people?' I realised that

that church had come into being, and Pastor Cho was able to handle the responsibility God had put on him, because he had put His relationship of love with the Lord uncompromisingly first. It came before anything else in life.

Sometimes when people come here, we ask them whether the Lord loves them – and one can learn where they are spiritually from their reply. Sometimes we go on and ask, 'And do you love Him?' Sometimes they brush the question aside as if to say, 'Yes, I do love Him, that's all right. Now let's get on with the next question.'

Often our reply has to be, 'But you do not love Him enough.' We are always safe saying that. Not one of us loves God – God who revealed Himself in Jesus – sufficiently. There needs to be in the heart of each of us a divine dissatisfaction with our love for Him. Often I find myself asking the Lord to forgive me for the weakness and the poverty of my love. Unless I surrender my ministry to Him and press on, ever seeking to love Him more and more with all my heart, there is no power in my ministry.

It is the same when people come to us saying confidently, 'Yes, I am a committed Christian.' When they say that, it is necessary for us very gently to ask if they are fully committed to Him. Who is? I long to be totally committed to the Lord but I know that there are still depths in my heart which Jesus hasn't yet been able to reach. As I look back over the years we have been at the London Healing Mission, I can say confidently that I am more committed to Him than I was six years ago. But I trust the Lord that six years from now I shall be even more committed than I am today. David Watson used to say, 'I am not what I ought to be. I am not what

I'm going to be. But, thank God, I am not what I was.'

Several of us from the mission were spending a few days helping a parish in south London. As we were having lunch with the vicar and his wife on the Sunday I remarked 'I find that I have to give myself afresh to the Lord every two or three months.' The vicar looked thoughtful. Then he turned to me and said, 'Well, Andy, I find that I need to give myself afresh to Him every day.'

How right he was. I have realised since then that I share the same need to commit my life afresh to Jesus every morning.

There is too much glib talk today about being committed Christians. I don't believe any of us will be fully committed to the Lord until the day comes when, to the singing of innumerable angels, we are ushered in through the gates of Heaven.

3
However do I Love God?

This brings us to the vital question, 'How do I love God?' How nice it would be if there were a simple answer. If we have been fortunate in our relationship with our earthly father, we may start to relate to God as being like an earthly father but infinitely more wonderful. But so many have had a poor relationship with an earthly father. The idea of father implies someone critical, angry and perhaps even cruel. So it is difficult to think of God in terms of being a father.

Many people feel caught in a trap. 'I have no feeling of love for God', they say. 'Therefore I cannot say I love God.' So long as they say that they cannot love God, they will be unable to love Him. We are set free from this trap when we realise that loving God starts with a decision to love, not with a feeling.

As we seek to love God there is a natural progression which we can follow. We start by saying thank you. When we say thank you to someone we are aware of being grateful. We may not love them but there is in us some sense of gratitude. All of us can sit and think of many, many things for which we can be thankful. We can thank Him that, unlike so many people, we have enough food. We can thank Him that, again unlike countless others, we have a sound roof over our heads and somewhere warm to live. We can thank Him that if we are caught out in the rain, almost without exception, we have another set of clothes into which we can change – this was rare among the men and women who lived in Jesus' day. We can thank Him for our family and friends. Maybe we are separated from our families, but usually there are at least a few acquaintances without whom our lives would be poorer.

We can thank Him for the use of our limbs or our eyes. I was praying a few days ago for a woman of forty who had an operation nine years before. She said the surgeon's knife had slipped and he had cut her spinal cord. She has been paralysed ever since. Audrey is ministering to a girl who knitted me a beautiful jersey last Christmas – yet who is totally blind. When did I last thank God for limbs and eyes? So we can go on. If we sit down and reflect, there is so much for which we can thank God.

Initially, there may be no feeling in this act of thanksgiving. It will be done as a decision, and indeed may seem mechanical, even like talking into empty air.

We are not asked to enter into a relationship of love with the Lord, relying upon our own efforts. It is essential to remember that there is, as it were, someone 'out there', someone who is real, though we can't see Him, and (this is the vital point) someone who is going to respond as we seek diligently to thank Him and to love Him.

If we make a practice of that prayer of thanksgiving – however mechanical it may seem – we shall find before long that we are meeting some response.

We shall become aware that we are not speaking to ourselves.

Once we have taken the decision to thank Him, then the pattern of our thankfulness can develop. We will thank God not just for the ways in which He has blessed us, but for who He is. Although we may not yet be able to feel His love, we know from the Bible that He is perfect love. We can thank Him for His love. We can consider how much He must be saddened by the selfishness and greed of mankind. We can thank Him for the patience He has with us. Perhaps we may remember some beautiful sunset when we were on holiday, and can thank Him for the beauty of creation. Perhaps we remember a particularly lovely butterfly, fluttering past us in the summer air. We can thank Him for that. We can remember how, when we recovered from that bad bout of 'flu, our strength gradually returned. We can thank Him that He is a God who heals.

Continue at this new level of thankful prayer, remembering all we have read about Him in the Bible, particularly in the gospel stories, and thanking Him for who He is. Soon our thanksgiving will become more joyful and we will begin to praise Him. As we praise God we will begin to love Him.

There is a natural progression from thanking God to praising Him. As we continue in our resolve to love Him, we will find we are entering into the intimacy of worship. Worship is a deeper expression of our love for Him.

Someone illustrated for me the difference between praise and worship. Some years ago, Queen Elizabeth the Queen Mother, celebrated her eightieth birthday. Early in the morning, a crowd gathered outside St

James' Palace, chanting happily, 'We want the Queen Mother! We want the Queen Mum!' There was nothing particularly personal in what they were calling out. They were just aware that they had come to express their appreciation of a remarkable lady who they all admired – even though probably none of them had met her personally. In religious terms the crowd were 'praising' her majesty.

Suppose you had been one of that crowd. Imagine, as you were standing there shouting for her majesty, you had seen the front door of the palace open. A splendidly uniformed footman made his way through the crowd and stopped in front of you. As he bowed he said, 'Her Majesty the Queen Mother would be graciously pleased if you would take tea with her.'

As you straightened your tie or applied some extra powder to your nose, your heart fluttered as you thought of this great honour. You followed the splendid figure of the footman through the front door of the palace and up the stairs. He throws open the door and announces your name to the Queen Mother.

As she beckons you forward, shows you to a chair and pours out tea, you are awestruck. No longer are you shouting to her with the crowd outside. Now, you are face to face, getting to know her and listening personally to her.

Worship is when we are aware of being in the presence of the One who is perfect love. We bask in the present of His love rather like someone enjoying the warmth of the sun on a fine day in summer. As we are filled with joy, our hearts open up and we pour our hearts out to Him in love. This is worship. Worship is an expression of our love for the Lord.

St John wrote, 'We love because He first loved us'

(1 Jn 4.19). We find at the Mission that much of the time we are trying to help people to receive for themselves the love of Jesus; to experience His love by thanking Him for it. Once we experience His love, then it is relatively easy to open our hearts and to love Him in return.

We remind people of what it was like when they were sunbathing last summer. They allowed the warmth of the sun to soak into their bodies while they lay there passively. An important element of prayer is allowing Him to minister to us, allowing ourselves to receive His love just as we allowed the warmth of the sun to soak into our bodies when we were sunbathing.

Alternatively, we can think of flowers. We have a goldfish pond in the middle of our lawn at home. The water lilies in it open their petals when the sun comes out. They don't 'do' anything else. They just remain with their petals open, drinking in the life-giving warmth of the sun.

It's the same with us when we pray. We just need to feel ourselves opening up and receiving into ourselves the life-giving love of Jesus.

It helps if we will use our imagination when praying. Indeed I believe using our imagination is a necessary part of prayer. We often help people to picture themselves with a lovely soft white light shining down on them from above. Our physical position helps too. We say 'Shut your eyes'. Sometimes people then bow their heads. We have been told in church, 'Bow your heads in prayer!' I don't think it is a good position. It is much more helpful, I believe, if we can raise our heads, with our eyes shut, and imagine ourselves looking up into His wonderful light.

We can hold our hands out too, not stiffly but loosely

and relaxed. The palms should be held upwards. We are a complex mixture of the physical and the spiritual. There seems an extra spiritual sensitivity in the palms of our hands. When we 'lay hands' on someone the palms face downwards.

We need to remember Jesus' own words, 'I am the Light . . .' (Jn 8.12). As we picture ourselves looking up into that light we realise that it is the embodiment of Jesus. Men and women down the centuries have seen Jesus as pure light.

Picture the light of Jesus shining full on you. Now go further and picture His light shining into you. Your heart is a room, perhaps rather musty and stuffy with windows that have been shut for years. Throw them open and allow the light of His love to glow in your heart.

As we become aware of the pure light of Jesus shining down into our hearts, we may be increasingly dissatisfied with ourselves. None of us is as good as we would like to be. None of us is unfailingly unselfish as we would like to believe. We fail to achieve our highest standards.

We can reflect on Jesus' words when the prostitute came up to Him as He reclined at a smart dinner party. She wept over Jesus' feet and dried them with her own hair. When his host objected, he replied that one who has been forgiven much will love much (Lk 7.47).

How far we fall short of the standard we would like to think we aim at. We can ask Jesus to forgive our failures. If necessary, we can go through them, one by one, asking His forgiveness. We can then accept His forgiveness, relying on those lovely words that 'if we confess our sins He is faithful . . . and will purify us from all unrighteousness' (1 Jn 1.9). We shall find that for us too, because we have been forgiven much we will also love much.

Someone said that the way to love God is by loving Him. Often our loving Him does not start with any feelings of love in our hearts at all. Our loving starts with our making the decision to love Him.

We can see a parallel in the love which flows between a husband and wife in a Christian marriage. In marriage, there are the three kinds of love – there is what the Greeks called the *eros* love, such as when his eyes meet hers in the candlelight and time stops still for them. Then there is the *philia* love, which is the love of two people who are friends and companions. The third love is the *agape* love, the love which takes the decision, the love which says, 'I am going to love the person I am married to.'

Many people have found in marriage counselling that, even if the marriage has broken down completely, if the two partners will take the decision with their wills to love each other, first the friendship love begins to come back, and then, in due course, all the fulness of the romantic love comes back too. It starts, though, with the *agape* love, namely the decision of the will that one is going to love the other person.

There is an exact parallel here with our loving the Lord. We need to take the decision to love Him. We may not feel any love for Him in our hearts, but that doesn't matter. If we take the decision, in obedience, that we are going to love Him, then, in time, the heartfelt love for Him will grow.

The other evening, after we had finished our ministry for the day, I was working at my desk when the doorbell rang. We have a rule that we see people only by appointment. But as I walked across the hall towards the front door I felt that familiar inner nudge. By the time my hand was on the door handle I was sure that I was going to have to see whoever had turned up unannounced on the doorstep.

I opened the door, and there was a young man from south-east Asia who was clearly in torment. He had turned up unannounced the previous week and I had told him to come to one of our healing services. Clearly he hadn't been helped. I asked him in.

He said he was a Christian and it was clear that he knew his Bible well. He knew too that Jesus' greatest commandment was for him to love God. But he said, 'I don't love God. I can't. I don't know how to love God.' It became clear that he felt he was therefore condemned to eternal damnation for breaking the most important commandment (Mt 22.37,38).

I explained to him that loving God was not a 'feeling' but it was simply a decision, taken consciously and deliberately and without emotion.

He shut his eyes and said, 'Jesus, I feel nothing for You, but in obedience to You I am taking the decision that from now onwards I'm going to love You.'

I told him to keep telling the Lord that he loved Him, and not to worry about feelings. I said that in weeks, or perhaps days, the feeling of loving the Lord might come to him.

How wrong I was. It took only minutes, and then quite oblivious to my presence I heard him saying over and over again, 'Jesus, You love me and Jesus, I love You. Jesus, You love me. Jesus, I love you.'

I can't remember how he went on, but I know that when he left he seemed to be about a foot taller, and he was filled with much joy.

In marriage it is important for each partner to tell the

other of their love. I am always delighted when Audrey tells me how much she loves me. We can't really expect to hear the Lord audibly telling us of His love, but we can thank Him continually that He does love us. Again, there need be no feeling of love in our hearts as we thank Him. But as our thanking Him for His love becomes part of our regular prayers so the awareness of that love begins to grow. The more we become aware of His love for us, the more we find that we are turning to Him and expressing our love for Him ourselves. We love Him because He first loved us.

When I tell my wife that I love her, I am expressing what is true. I do love her. At the same time, the more I tell her that I love her, the more my love for her actually grows. I don't know which comes first – it's a chicken-and-egg situation!

In exactly the same way, we tell the Lord that we love Him. The more we tell Him, the more our love for Him will actually grow.

There is a connection between loving Him and being obedient. St John writes, 'This is love for God: to obey His commands' (1 Jn 5.3). We are obedient to God because we love Him – it is also true that we love him because we are obedient to Him. The two go together.

Neither is easy. It is not easy to love God, nor is it easy to obey Him. But if Jesus Himself has told us that the most important thing in life is to love God, then surely it is worth working at it. Sometimes people claim that it is easy to be a Christian. That isn't true. Jesus Himself described the easy way through life, and where did He say it led? To destruction. 'Small is the gate and narrow the road which leads to life' (Mt 7.14). It is not easy to follow Him but it is never too hard if we will really try. It is the only way to live life to the full.

Perhaps there is a further lesson we can learn from the marriage relationship. When we are with someone we are fond of, it seems natural to share what we are thinking with them. We need to get into the way of sharing similarly with the Lord all through the day. When we are alone we can share what we are thinking with Him. We can bring to Him any thought that comes into our minds. We can treat Him as we would a close and intimate friend.

Other people can help us to love Him. In many churches nowadays there are small groups of people, perhaps only three or four, who meet in one of their homes on a weekday evening to pray together. If we can join such a group, where the other members know the Lord and love Him, as we hear them talking in prayer and relating to Him, we learn instinctively how to do so ourselves and how to love Him.

In a similar way, if we go to a church where the people are accustomed to praising the Lord from their hearts, perhaps singing some of the lovely modern choruses of praise and worship, we will find that as we join in the singing, we too get caught up, perhaps without realising what is happening, and start expressing our love for Him in worship.

Once we have begun to experience that expression of love in the company of others, we can grow into that same relationship, in our own times of prayer with the Lord.

The story is told of a vicar who went to a new parish. There was a good turn-out on the first Sunday, as everyone wanted to meet him, and perhaps to know if he was a good preacher. They were not disappointed. He preached a splendid sermon on Jesus' words that the first and greatest commandment is to love God.

Everyone went home after the service, and told their friends enthusiastically, 'We've got a really good new vicar and he preaches very well.'

The following Sunday the church was fuller than ever. When it came to the time for the sermon, as the vicar mounted the steps to the pulpit, everyone was sitting forward in anticipation. To their surprise he preached the same sermon again.

'He must be a bit absent-minded,' they said as they left the church. 'Perhaps he forgot that he preached that sermon last Sunday.'

The following Sunday everyone wondered what his subject would be. As his sermon unfolded, they realised that he was preaching the original sermon once again.

Afterwards one of the churchwardens took him aside. 'Vicar,' he said, 'that was a good sermon. A really good sermon.' He paused. 'But, vicar,' he said, 'you will be preaching a different sermon next Sunday, won't you?'

'No!' the vicar replied. 'I'm going to go on preaching about the need for them to love God until they actually do it!'

I cannot guarantee that the story is true. What I do know, however, is that very often a preacher will have one special theme in his preaching and, whatever the subject he announces, he will come back to what, for him, is the central theme of his faith. If Jesus Himself said that the first and greatest rule in life is to love the Lord our God with all our heart, with all our soul, with all our mind and with all our strength (Mk 12.30) then that should be central in our lives.

4
'When I Pray
I Laugh with Jesus'

Jesus did not say that we were just to love the Lord. He said we were to put our relationship of love with Him first and foremost in our lives. To put aside half an hour or so each day for reading the Bible and prayer is all that we are usually capable of doing. For most people, it is all He asks.

We need first to work out, perhaps by trial and error, what is the right length of time for us to devote to being in the direct presence of our Lord. It has been said that everyone needs to spend not less than half an hour each day with the Lord, except, it has been stressed, when we are very busy. Then, the minimum amount of time for us to spend with the Lord is three-quarters of an hour.

There is truth in this seemingly contradictory remark. If we skimp our time of prayer we will miss out on that peace of God which is beyond human understanding, that peace which He so longs to give us. If we have been resolute about making our time with the Lord a top priority, and for as long as He wants, then when we finish, we shall be resting in His peace. That inner peace will go with us through the day. We will find at the end of the day that we have actually got through more than if we had cut down on our time of prayer.

For some, however, the problem is the opposite. Those who live alone, or perhaps are unemployed, find that the problem is having not too little time but too much. I believe then it is just as important for us to have a set finishing time for prayer, as it is to have a starting time. Unless we discipline ourselves to work to some pattern, we shall go on putting off our time of prayer, always saying to ourselves, 'Well, I've still got plenty of time to pray.' When eventually we get down to it, we shall probably be too tired to make a success of it. Set a time to cease praying as well to start – and stick to both.

Few ever reach the point in prayer where the mind never wanders off. I believe the Lord can speak to us during those moments when we have forgotten what we are doing and we find ourselves thinking of something quite different. Once we realise that our attention has strayed, I find it helpful to take the last thought that has been in my mind and turn it into a prayer and thus come back into His presence. We may have found ourselves reliving that moment yesterday when somebody wasn't very kind to us. Their words were slighting and hurtful. Take that thought, and lift it up to Jesus offering Him the hurt and asking Him to heal and give us back His peace.

We may find ourselves thinking of how we flared up in anger. Again we can bring that straight to Jesus as a prayer, asking Him to forgive us for having hit back at the one who hurt us. Once again we come back into His presence.

As our minds wander during prayer, we may find ourselves thinking of something as mundane as the car needing servicing. Turn it into a prayer. Scribble down a reminder, and thank Jesus that in His love he has called to your mind that very thing which you had nearly forgotten.

A way of entering into His presence which has helped many is to read aloud a passage about Jesus in one of the gospel stories. Reflect on the story you have read. Use your imagination and fill in all the details which have been omitted. Think of the deep blue of the sub-tropical sky. Describe the heat and the dust, and the slight wind that blows through the hilly country-side. Picture the grey-green leaves of the olive trees and their gnarled trunks. Consider the goats wandering individually, seeking a patch of grazing here and a few leaves there. Picture the skinny chickens scratching in the dust for grubs.

Go on to picture Jesus walking along the dusty track, deep in conversation with His disciples, or with a group of hangers-on following loosely behind. Perhaps a blind man from the side of the road calls out (Mk 10.46,47). Jesus asks that they bring him to Him. Sense the atmosphere as the crowd gathers, waiting to hear what He says. There is a hush, an air of expectancy: 'Is He going to heal his blindness? Will He make the man see?' Experience the tension yourself. As Jesus puts His hands on the man's eyes, the man gives a shout and pandemonium breaks loose. He's healed. For the first time in his life he can see. He goes delirious with joy and thankfulness. See the crowd patting Jesus on the back saying how wonderful He is healing the blind man.

As we fill in the detail of the story think about what is going on in Jesus' mind, of the expression on His face. It seems that whatever was going on around Him, Jesus was calm and filled with an inner peace. He was completely in control of every situation. Describe the compassion in His face, the peace, the tenderness – and the power. With the man healed imagine Jesus lifting up His own heart to Heaven amid the hubbub around Him. Imagine Him communing silently with His Father, knowing there is joy in heaven too.

If we use our imagination in this way as we read one of the gospel stories, we finish by being caught up in the same joyful worship as the crowd around Jesus.

Between the wars, the Rev Studdert Kennedy taught thousands of people to pray through picturing stories from the gospel. He encouraged them to have a little room where they could withdraw and meet with Jesus. Some are helped by picturing the door to that little room. We use our imagination to see what it is like to go through the door, and find ourselves in that room which we share with Jesus. We picture how the room is furnished, the colour of the carpet and the walls, and 'see' any pictures there may be. We picture what it is like to be there with Jesus sitting on one chair and one-self on the other. The door is shut so that the two of us are alone together, enjoying the other's company to the full.

I remember one of the very few occasions when I have fallen to the floor under the power of the Holy Spirit. It was in the middle of the aisle in an Anglican church in the City of London. Several fell in turn as the preacher that day laid hands on each of us. We must have presented an untidy spectacle, lying at all angles in that broad church aisle!

I don't know what the Lord did in the lives of the others but, for me, it was one of the most wonderful experiences. I don't know whether I was there a few seconds, or many minutes. I was oblivious of every-thing else except Jesus. People were stepping over us, like so many logs on the ground, but I was unaware. For those precious moments I had the whole of Jesus' attention and He had the whole of mine. There was lightness, joy and companionship with One who loved me with a perfect love. We can bring that same experience to mind as we picture ourselves in our little room with Jesus.

The main object of prayer for each of us is to enter in this way into the presence of Jesus. Of course, intercession comes into prayer, both for ourselves and for others. But the central act in prayer must, I feel sure, be worship.

How do we enter into His presence and into that relationship of love and worship? It is not always the same key which is needed to unlock the door of that inner room. We have various needs. The Lord may bring to our mind some aspect of our life which dishonours Him. There may be the need to receive His cleansing, to surrender ourselves afresh to Him. He may want us to trust Him more completely. He may be looking for more obedience in us, so that we may follow Him more closely.

On a particular morning, any one of these prayers may be the key which opens the door for me to come into His presence, but there may be others. Often I come into His presence just repeating over and over the two words of adoration, 'Jesus, Lord!' One can get many shades of meaning into those two words.

At other times a repeated expression of my deepest needs may bring me into His presence, and I find myself praying, 'Lord, all I want is to love You, to trust You, to follow You.'

Sometimes, when I first wake up and try to pray, I find that I am battling with sleep, and struggling to regain full consciousness so that I may worship Him. I may be too sleepy to hear how the Holy Spirit is leading me. If one has the gift of a spiritual language, it can be helpful. As I use my will to pray in the language of the Holy Spirit, the clouds gradually clear away, and once again I move into the presence of Jesus.

What is our aim? We need to know that in our time of prayer we are seeking to come into His direct presence, into that relationship of love and worship with Him. We need to be pressing forward to that position where we are alone with Jesus, each giving our full attention to the other and each enjoying the other's company. We need to practise being open to the Holy Spirit, as He shows us in which direction we should pray, so that we may open that door and move into His presence.

Once we are in the presence of Jesus, it is easy! We just can't stop telling Him how much we love Him and expressing our joy at being with Him.

Many suffer from loneliness. One household in eight consists of a person living alone. It has been said that the one cure for loneliness is to pray for others. Usually, if we look out of our window, we can see people. If we are in the unusual situation where we can't see anyone, we can turn on our television set and see people. It is a wonderful help for the lonely to sit in front of the window and pray for every person who passes by. The fact that we don't know them individually does not matter. Jesus loves each one of them as much as He loves us. Some will have no-one to pray for them. As we lift them up to Jesus in prayer, we are bringing joy to His heart and blessing to them. How true it is that in blessing others we ourselves are blessed.

Very few of us are called to spend all our time in prayer. Agnes Sanford, a forerunner of the return of the healing ministry to the Church, says in one of her books that she is a busy housewife and mother and just hasn't the time to spend long hours in prayer. If we are to be completely surrendered to the Lord, and if we are to seek to put our relationship of love with Him before anything else in this life, how are we to put that into practical effect?

The first step must be to have our time of prayer with the Lord. Then we will go quietly through the day remaining in His presence. We will find that, little by little, He is leading us and prompting us. We will find that it becomes easier, whatever we are doing, to do it for Him and out of love for Him. We will find that almost instinctively we are seeking to do everything as well as we possibly can for His sake. Thus, although we have spent only a small proportion of the day in actual prayer, we are living in His presence right through the day. Then when we go to bed we can sink back, tired but thankful, thanking Him for the way He has been with us all through the day.

There is a lovely prayer which we can pray at any time during a busy day. It is a prayer which has no words, and we can 'pray' it even in the middle of a conversation. We can just picture ourselves as small children lifting up our hands and holding on to Jesus' hand. Then we feel safe with Him, and we can enjoy a renewed awareness of His being with us.

A middle-aged woman first came to us at the Mission with a history of considerable mental disturbance. Recently, she wrote us this letter about prayer:

> You know I don't sleep very well. So I spend a long time in *quite private* prayers. I start to talk to Jesus about my day, from getting up to going to bed. I thank Him for the good bits. I'm always surprised how many good moments I've had. And I say sorry for the slip-ups.

Then I tell Jesus about the people or things I'm worried about, and ask Him what I should do about them. I ask Him about the next day, and to be with me to help me.

After each little bit I've learned to be still, to listen very hard sometimes, for quite a long time, and say 'Jesus' very quietly.

Then it comes. I feel an answer. God speaks to me, not in words, just a sort of feeling, sad or happy, comforting, positive, laughing, all kinds of feelings. I can't really describe it, just deep, deep down inside, and it feels so good. I'm so glad God is not only the creator, all-powerful, but also that He is Jesus, who is my friend.

I'm not afraid of anyone, any illness, or anything, any more.

In many ways prayer is just enjoying being with Jesus. The story is told of a little boy aged four who, as is common with little boys, would think up every excuse he could as soon as his mother started telling him that it was time to go to bed.

Then one evening, to her great surprise, when she told him it was bedtime, he didn't hesitate but immediately started packing up his toys and trotted off happily to bed. She couldn't believe her eyes! She wondered what would happen the following evening.

Sure enough, exactly the same thing happened – and again the evening after that. When she went up to say goodnight to her little son in bed, she couldn't help saying to him, 'Johnny, it's lovely that you are so obedient now and you go up to bed as soon as I tell you. What has made the change in you?'

Her curiosity was, if anything, increased when her small son replied, 'I like going up to bed now, because I can say my prayers.'

The mother paused. 'What do you actually say when you say your prayers?' she asked.

'Oh, I don't say anything,' came the reply, 'I just kneel by my bed with Jesus, and we laugh and laugh together.'

That story is a wonderful description of real prayer. Real prayer is being in the presence of Jesus, being filled with His joy and the happiness of being with him.

5
But What does He really Want?

Someone once said that when the high-churchman prays, he feels he has to draw God's attention to what He really ought to be getting on with. But when the low-churchman prays, he accepts that God knows what He ought to be doing, but seeks to twist God's arm, to press Him to get a move on.

It is easy for us to smile, but how many of us can truthfully say that we have never had similar thoughts? There have been situations which we felt God must have overlooked, and we have felt it imperative for us to draw them to His attention.

Yet God is all-knowing. God is all-loving. He is all-powerful. He is always longing to help, to comfort, to heal, and to make whole. What, therefore, are we seeking to achieve by interceding with Him?

Two key verses when we consider praying effectively are in 1 John: 'If we ask anything according to His will, He hears us. And if we know that He hears us – whatever we ask – we know that we have what we have asked of Him' (1 Jn 5.14, 15).

Often it helps to read a passage in more than one

translation. Paraphrase may convey more of what the writer actually had in his mind. In the Living Bible these two verses are rendered: 'We are sure of this, that He will listen to us whenever we ask Him for anything in line with His will. And if we really know He is listening when we talk to Him and make our requests, then we can be sure that He will answer us.'

I believe that intercessory prayer is the process of releasing the power of God to do what He has been longing to do anyway. But why does He wait for us to pray, before He does it?

God has given us free will. How deeply it must grieve His heart to see how we misuse that free will in our selfishness and our greed. Yet He has given us free will because He longs to have each person's heart surrendered to Him in perfect love. You can never force anybody to love you. God can't force us to love Him. We have to be free to love Him or to reject Him. Thus God has set us free.

I would not want to forego that free will. Without it, I would be a zombie. I would no longer be a real person. However much I know that I misuse it, I am thankful for the free will God has given me. I am glad to be able to turn to Him of my own free will and to give Him the love which otherwise I could not give Him. I treasure the freedom He has given me.

But part of the freedom He has given us lies in the fact that, in many cases, God has voluntarily restricted His own power until such time as we turn to him in prayer, and pray to Him in line with His will. It is when we discern what His will is, in a particular situation, and when we pray in line with His will, that we release His power to do what He has been longing to do all the time.

There are two points in these verses in 1 John 5. The

first stresses the importance of praying in line with His will. Then come the words. 'And if we *know* that He hears us . . .' We need to have faith.

Never say, however, if there is not an instantaneous healing when we pray for someone, that it is their fault for not having had enough faith. It may be because our own faith has been lacking. It may well be that the Lord wanted to release a gradual, or a delayed, healing – and such healings are far more common than the immediate ones. If we imply that a person has not been healed because of their own lack of faith, they will leave us in a worse state. To their continuing sickness we have now added a burden of guilt. This is not love.

But I do believe that two most important points when we seek to pray effectively are, first, discerning what God is anyway longing to do and, second, having the faith to believe He will do it. The two are linked.

What is it that God is longing to do? We need first to consider that question from a general point of view. Then we can look at it more particularly, depending on our situation.

God is perfect. If He was anything less He would be like one of us. We might admire Him but we could never worship Him. We could never give Him the love of our hearts. We can do that only when we reflect that in every way He is perfect.

It must follow therefore that when He created the world He must have made it perfect. Indeed that is what we read in Genesis. When God had finished His creation He looked at His handiwork and saw that it was very good. Of course it was, because the God who is perfect had created it (Gen 1.31).

Something of the creator goes into all creative work.

Whether it be a painting, a piece of music, or a sculpture, you will see in it something of the character and nature of the person who brought it into being. The same must be true of God. A God who is perfect could only have brought into being a world which was perfect.

But then there was the fall (Gen 3). We don't know what happened at the fall. Whether you take literally the story of a serpent who conversed with a young woman, tempting her to eat an apple, or whether you take it as an allegory, it is the only explanation I know which reconciles the existence of a God of perfect love with all the sin and suffering that there is in the world today. Somehow, at the time of the fall, Satan got in and spoilt God's perfect handiwork. Sin and suffering, sickness and pain, entered into the world.

What then has been the longing in the heart of God from that day to this? It must follow that He is longing to make His creation perfect once again.

A few years ago, Audrey and I were on holiday in the Auvergne, a little known mountainous region in the centre of France. We both enjoy painting in water colours. After a rainy morning we went out to paint the little village square. By my side was a large and muddy puddle. We started to paint and a crowd of children soon gathered round us. My French is far from perfect, but I could understand the comments. 'That's my dad's front door and it isn't that colour', 'That's my bedroom window and you've drawn it wrong', and 'My grandma's awning doesn't look like that.' I wondered what I would have said if one of them had knocked the paper off my knee and it had fallen face downwards in the puddle. The colours would have run and the picture would have been ruined.

I know what I would have done. I would have taken the painting back to the hotel. I would very carefully have sponged the mud off it, and I would then have tried to recreate as good a picture as I could, out of the ruin of the one which had been spoilt.

Isn't that an illustration of how God must be feeling? Having created a world which in every way was perfect, as He wanted it to be, and then having seen it spoilt at the time of the fall, mustn't He be longing to perfect His creation once again? By His very nature, God is always longing to comfort each of us whom He loves so dearly. He wants to be allowed to guide us so that we may say no to our sinful selves and thus enter more and more fully into His wonderful joy and His peace. He yearns to release us from the pain of past hurts, to set us free from the bondages of bad habits and sin, and to heal us in body and soul, mind and spirit, so that at the end He may have His glorious way and we may once again be perfect.

We need to remember, too, that God is outside time. Our life in this world is only the beginning. Winston Churchill used to describe death as 'the end of the beginning'. We need to remember that God is longing for the time when, at some stage after death, we are ushered into the glory of His direct presence to be with Him in joy, for ever.

However, as we reflect on the wonderful holiness of God and his awesome presence, we realise how far we fall short of His standard. We know that we are still sinful human beings. Then as we reflect, we realise the truth in the Old Testament, that God cannot look on sin (Hab 1.13). If any sin were to come into the direct presence of that blinding holiness, it would just shrivel up and cease to exist. If God is to have His way and we

are to come into His direct presence, we must ourselves
be holy, or else we too will shrivel up and cease to exist.
When the time comes for us to enter heaven, we must be
perfect like our Heavenly Father. We must be holy like
God. At the end of Matthew 5, we read Jesus' words,
'Be perfect, therefore, as your Heavenly Father is perfect' (Mt 5.48), while in Peter's first letter, we read 'Be
holy . . . just as the Lord is holy' (1 Pet 1.15, Living
Bible).

God is longing for us to allow Him to perfect His
creation in us during our time in this world. That
process is never completed during our earthly lifetimes.
No man or woman has yet been born who before dying
was perfect – excepting only Jesus. But the process is
begun in this life and the culmination comes after
death. We don't know the details of how or when, but
we read in 1 Corinthians 15, that 'in the twinkling of an
eye' we shall all be changed and then at last we shall be
ready to enter the gates of heaven. Then at last we shall
ourselves be like God.

Thus God views us from the standpoint of eternity.
So often we pray for the wrong things because we see
things only from a human view, in the course of our life
in this world. How different is our view from God's.
Indeed, as He Himself has said, 'As the heavens are
higher than the earth, so are My ways higher than your
ways' (Is 55.9). As we pray we need to discern what
His will is, when viewed against the backdrop of
eternity.

His longing is to make us whole. One of the meanings
of the Greek word *sozo*, (from which we get 'salvation'),
is 'wholeness'. This means being perfect in body, soul,
mind and spirit.

This must be the yearning of a God of perfect love.

But how do we discern His will in any specific situation in which we may find ourselves? In the unfolding of His wonderful plan, the Lord always knows what the next step is in the life of each one of us, as He continues His work of perfecting His creation in us. We need to discern that next step if we are to pray effectively. He often does reveal this to us. He is not leaving us just to battle on on our own, but loves us and is longing to help us and to do what is the very best for us.

I can think of two separate occasions when a particular sin in the life of the person we were praying for was revealed to one of us as we ministered. In one case it was the sin of bitterness and resentment. In the other person, it was a sexual sin committed some forty years earlier. Both people had physical problems, but we knew this only in the first case.

On both occasions, we shared with the person concerned the sin which the Lord had shown us. Each accepted that it was a sin which needed forgiveness. In each case there was a lovely prayer of repentance, followed by a shout of joy as the physical problem was then healed immediately – before we had prayed for it! I am convinced that if we had not been listening to what the Lord was saying in prayer, and if we had just prayed for the physical healing, that prayer would not have been answered. How strong then would have been the temptation to relapse into saying, 'Well obviously God didn't want to heal this person'.

We had a lovely example of a word of knowledge quite recently. The London Healing Mission is shut on Sundays – partly because we do not want to compete with churches, but also because so often Audrey and I are travelling around preaching and ministering. Consequently, the team here worship at churches in the places where they live. During a Sunday service, Robin, (one of our team), felt a pain in his left kidney and got up at the end of the service and said, 'There is someone here with a pain in their left kidney which the Lord wants to heal.' A strapping young man came up to him, saying 'That's me.' He had an infection in his left kidney and the following day his consultant was deciding what was to be done. His right kidney had been removed the previous year.

Several of them prayed for him. He fell under the power of the Holy Spirit and rested in great peace upon the floor. His parents had not seen this happen before and started getting agitated. Eventually, after twenty minutes, they said they really must take him home to lunch, and with some sadness the young man got up and went with them.

It was later that week that a mutual friend rang Robin to tell him that the young man had seen his consultant the following day. 'There is no infection in the left kidney', the consultant had said. '*Both* kidneys are working perfectly.'

The Lord had indicated through a word of knowledge the next thing He wanted to do in that young man's life, to perfect His creation in him. We continually see God revealing what He wants to do next in a particular person's life.

Ray is another member of our team. At the end of a healing service in our chapel, he said, 'I believe the Lord has given me a word of knowledge about someone He wants to heal now. But,' he went on, 'I can't quite make it out. The name seems to be Peterson, but I'm sure the last three letters are SEN.' A woman got up at the back of the chapel. 'My name is Petersen,' she said, 'but I spell it the Danish way, and the last three letters of my name are SEN.' She came to the front for prayer and the Lord healed her.

When Audrey and I were leading a healing weekend in Yorkshire, we had asked Jesus to release the power of His Holy Spirit upon the hundred or so people in the hall. Audrey saw the Holy Spirit falling powerfully on one woman – and this was not the time to ask her why she wanted prayer! As Audrey listened to what the Lord was saying she prayed that the woman might be set free from anything wrong that had come to her from previous generations, and she found herself putting her hand on the woman's spine and praying. After the service the woman came up to Audrey with a broad smile. 'Who told you', she asked, 'that my problem was an hereditary back pain?'

There must be many times when I have failed to hear what the Lord is saying. Often He prompts us but we don't recognise His voice. There must be times too when I am mistaken in what I think I'm hearing. However, I can't get it wrong every time or else no-one would get healed! And we do see many people being healed. As we minister to people here, whether listening to all they want to tell us or praying with them, we need at the same time to be listening attentively with that 'third ear' to what the Lord may be telling us.

We need to be expecting the Lord to disclose to us what He wants to do. Thus we need to be open to any gentle, inner prompting that may come to us, whether it be a thought or words, or by a picture. I believe we are more likely to discern what He is trying to say to us if we keep our eyes on the Lord Himself. Let me illustrate this from wartime days when we were being trained in the army for night fighting.

At night it can be a matter of life or death for a soldier

whether he can discern in the dim starlight if something in front of him is just a shadow, or whether there is an enemy there. We were taught that if we looked directly we would discern less than if we looked to one side. It has to do with the retina of the eye. The retina is less sensitive in the centre than round the edges. Astronomers call it 'averted vision'.

If we are seeking to discern what God is saying to us in a particular situation, we need to look away from the problem and look to Jesus. Then we are more likely to be receptive to what he is seeking to disclose to us.

There is another way. Very often when I am praying with someone, I simply don't know how to pray or what to pray for. I may have already been praying for five or ten minutes, and I have, as it were, 'run out of prayer'. I find then that if I switch to the language of the Holy Spirit, by using what the Bible calls 'the gift of tongues', the Lord then gives me the English. I pray in the English until that runs out. Then I switch back into this language, and He gives me the further words in English which He wants me to pray. Invariably when one switches into that language of the Holy Spirit, one is aware of a fresh access of spiritual power. Sometimes I then find myself saying in prayer, 'I take complete control of this situation in the Name of Jesus!'

But there is another and very practical way of discerning the Lord's will. When we are uncertain of what He wants, put the straight question to Him! It has been said that often the first thought which comes into our minds when we do this is from the Lord, the second thought is from ourselves, and the third, if we pause that long, may well be from Satan.

This does not always work. But if we are turning to the Lord in prayer and asking a straight question, it is

quite logical, since we have entered into prayerful
communion with Him, for the first thought to be from
Him. Then as we hesitate, the doubts begin to come in.
We are less involved with him in prayer and the errant
human self starts coming up with a different thought.
By that time the doubts have really taken hold of us. We
have taken our eyes right off the Lord and Satan has his
go.

Audrey and I were praying for a woman in her early
thirties who had been desperately rejected as a child.
She never knew her real father and whenever anything
went wrong her mother would always blame her,
saying, 'Well, it's all your fault. I never wanted you
anyway.' (Add to that the fact that the girl had been
seduced by her minister and) it was clear that she was in
great need.

As we spoke with her, we heard the unclean spirits
within her actually speaking out. What interested me,
though, was that both Audrey and I were conscious
that the Lord was saying, 'Heal her, heal her.' If we had
tried to get rid of the unclean spirits during that session,
I don't believe they would have gone, as that was not
the next step in God's will for that girl. So often
deliverance and healing go together, and it is essential
to follow where the Lord is leading, in order that His
power may be released according to His perfect plan.

But how does He heal? Perhaps I should make it
clear straight away, that in thus using the word 'heal' I
am thinking of it in the sense of God's ultimate purpose
of making us whole and perfect. It may be that at a
particular time for each one of us, the next thing He
longs to do is to heal us spiritually. This may involve
repentance for some sin and the consequent forgiveness. It may be that the next thing He longs to be

allowed to do is to heal us from some deep emotional hurt we suffered in the past. Again it may be that His next step is to heal us of some mental or physical sickness. We are wonderfully made with body, mind, soul and spirit interlocking and inter-reacting. He may want to bring healing and wholeness to several parts of our being.

But what is His method? How does He heal?

We gave much thought to this when Audrey and I were first asked to write a book about our work here. Eventually we decided to call it *Love that Heals* because it is His love which does heal. If we can help people to open their hearts to Him, to receive for themselves His wonderful love, and then be led to release themselves to Him as they return His love, then His healing can flow into them.

I have an electric lamp in my room. To illustrate my point, I sometimes unplug the lamp from the socket and I then make great play of turning the switch on and off. Nothing, of course, happens. I then ostentatiously plug the lamp into the socket, turn the switch and of course the light comes on. That lamp does not light up unless it is connected to the power supply and the electrical circuit is thus completed.

I believe it is the same with each of us and the Lord. If we can help someone to receive the love of Jesus then it is fairly easy for them to start to love Him themselves. They can then think of Jesus receiving their love and pouring out more of His love on them. They then receive more of His love and they in turn love Him the more. Jesus gratefully and joyfully receives the stronger flow of their love, and more of His love pours down upon them. Thus a continuing circuit of love is established, us and Jesus each loving the other and each receiving the other's love. His power to heal flows as this circuit of love is established and grows stronger.

In our earlier book we wrote about Virginia. She had come to us in her late thirties, having been a manic depressive for 25 years. In her case it was Audrey who ministered to her and she was healed completely in a few weeks. Soon after, she came to join us as one of the team here.

Because of her depression, Virginia had never been able to form a stable relationship and she had her first boyfriend when she was forty. A year later, they got married. When they had been married for a year that I said to Virginia, 'Surely you've been married long enough to know that Jesus must always come first in your life, and not Michael?' Virginia thought for a few minutes and then looked up at me, kindly, but with the look a grown-up has when a child asks a silly question. 'Of course I know,' Virginia replied, 'that if I become unplugged from Jesus I'm no use to Michael.' The more we can 'plug in' to that wonderful circuit of love, the more the Lord's power to heal is released into us, and out through us to other people.

The story is still told of how St John was preaching one day, in his old age. He was preaching about love. At the end, a young man came up to him. 'Father John,' he asked, 'why are you always talking about love?'

'There is only love,' the old disciple replied. As he had written earlier in one of his letters, 'God is love.'

6

Some of Our Difficulties

A vicar told me how the Lord was healing people in his parish. 'But,' he added, 'you must remember that there are only two hundred people in the congregation and we are not all ill, all the time!'

Because of our specialised work, as a team, we pray individually for well over a hundred people each week, (though many of them will come more than once). We must learn something from all the experience which the Lord gives us here!

I am always conscious that Jesus loves each one of us with a love which is unique. He never takes the 'broad brush' approach. Yet a problem will often come up which we have met earlier with some-one else. Indeed we find that some problems crop up repeatedly. In this chapter we look at some of them.

Sometimes Christians come to us complaining that they are under great attack from Satan. In every area of their lives they are conscious of Satan troubling them, tormenting them and tempting them. How can they get free? Sometimes they will say, 'I keep on rebuking him and telling him to get behind me, but he always comes back again!'

We need to remember that when Jesus had occasion to speak sternly to Peter, saying, 'Get thee behind me, Satan!' (AV), He matched His actions to His words. If we read the account of that episode carefully in Mark's Gospel (Mk 8.33) we see that as Jesus spoke those words He turned back to His disciples, and thus physically turned His back on Peter. Indeed the more accurate NIV translation quotes Jesus as saying to Peter, 'Out of my sight, Satan!'

As we rebuke Satan, we need deliberately to turn our backs on him. Instead of that, so many people immediately look behind them to see that he is there. If Satan is behind us we cannot see him and, even more to the point, he is out of our minds. Then as we turn fully to face Jesus, our whole vision can be taken up with Him. We need to turn away from Satan and to face the glorious light of Jesus.

Satan is real. If Satan wasn't real, then one could almost argue that Jesus' sacrifice of Himself upon the cross was a waste of time. After all, the story of the cross is that as He shed His blood for us, freely, and out of pure love, He won an immense and final victory over Satan. Ever since then Satan has been the defeated enemy. Satan is real – but don't let us spare a thought for him.

A woman came to see me who had been once before. 'I've been under such attack from Satan,' she said. 'No sooner had I left your mission than I was very nearly run over by a car. It had to swerve violently to avoid hitting me.' She saw this as Satan attacking her.

'Did you ever think,' I asked, 'of thanking Jesus that His hand was on you all the time? Did you think of thanking Jesus that He protected you so that that dangerous driver was not able to touch you?' It hadn't occurred to her to look at the episode that way!

Much the same is true where our problems are concerned. Many people come to us who are 'problem-centred'. We have to help them to get their eyes off their problems and on to Jesus.

I was making this point in our chapel in a healing service. 'Look round to your left,' I said. What they saw was the back of their neighbour's head. I then asked them to look to their right and again in most cases what they saw was the back of somebody else's head. 'Now look at both heads at the same time,' I asked.

Of course, they couldn't. It is the same with us and our problems. Either we look at our problems or we look at Jesus. We cannot look at both at the same time. We need to get our eyes off our problems and on to Jesus.

Imagine that we are out walking on the Downs on a lovely summer's day. We can imagine the grass fresh and springy under our feet, the sun shining from a cloudless sky and the larks singing overhead. We can imagine ourselves walking up a valley. Far away, at the end of the valley we can see a tiny dot. We know that's a farmhouse and that when we get there, having by then worked up a really good appetite, there will be a lovely lunch waiting for us. However, as we round the shoulder of a hill, we are brought to a halt. There has been a landslide. The way ahead is blocked. We can no longer see the farmhouse.

We then have two alternatives. Either we can stand there looking at the landslide as it blocks our path and bewail our misfortune. Alternatively, we can scramble uphill (or downhill) until we have worked our way round the landslide. Then, once again, we will be able to see our goal and we can resume our progress towards it.

Substitute our problems for the landslide and Jesus for the farmhouse. It is no use just standing there looking at our problems and bewailing them. We need resolutely to look past our problems to Jesus. Then our problems come into proportion and they seem less menacing. Even more important, we resume our contact with Jesus, and He then helps us to move on past our problems and to leave them behind us. We look to Jesus by a decision of the will.

Much the same is true over negative thoughts. Audrey and I still catch ourselves thinking negatively from time to time, and many people come here filled with negative thoughts. A man poured out his woes to me the other day. Eventually I said to him, 'Do you realise that while we've been talking I've tried repeatedly to bring you to the solution of your problems, whereas you have each time directed me back to the problems?'

The moment we catch ourselves thinking a negative thought we need to turn to Jesus and thank Him for the opposite. I may find myself concerned for one of the family who is ill. Instead of worrying that they are not getting better, I need to turn at once to Jesus and thank Him that He has the situation completely in His hands, and that He is healing that person in His own perfect timing.

I may be worried about something which I must do in the future. Will I know what to do when the time comes? Will I be able to handle the situation? Negative doubts begin to set in. I need then to turn to Jesus and thank Him, 'Thank You, Jesus, that I know that You are going to be with me, that You will be guiding me, and helping me.'

A large and unexpected bill may come through our letter-box. Our immediate thought is that this will upset our family budget. How are we going to manage financially? Again we need resolutely to turn to Jesus, to dismiss the fear and praise Him, 'Thank You, Jesus, that You have promised that if we seek Your Kingdom first You will provide for us in all material needs' (see Mt 6.33).

Satan attacks through filtering negative thoughts into our minds. I believe that his favourite weapon is fear. I used to think that the opposite of love was hatred, but I have come to see that it is fear. Moreover, when we talk to people who have themselves been deep into Satanic worship, we realise how fear has permeated the whole of their thinking.

There is a devilish progression which starts with fear. Many of us would not admit to being full of fear. The more respectable words are 'worry' or 'anxiety'. People don't go to their doctor, saying, 'I'm full of fear.' But they will often go saying, 'I'm afraid I'm an awful worrier. I'm very anxious.' 'Worry' and 'anxiety' are only different words for the underlying feeling of fear.

There is then a progression from worry or anxiety to tension and then on to stress. As we allow worry to take hold, and we become anxious, so we lose the peace of God. Thus tension builds up in us. What the Lord wants more than anything is for us to have that wonderful relationship of love with Him, but you cannot love anybody, whether man or woman, or indeed God, if you don't first trust them. Once we allow Satan to disrupt our trust in the Lord and instead to feed thoughts of worry or anxiety into our unconscious minds, then he has managed to get between us and Jesus. Once that happens, he can start having his destructive way with us.

When we are suffering from tension or stress, we are laying ourselves open to all manner of illnesses. Doctors have quoted percentages from fifty to as high as ninety for the proportion of illnesses which are made worse by stress, if not actually brought on by it. Stress can lead to pains in the shoulders and the neck, to headaches and migraine, to digestive problems, to heart troubles, arthritis and rheumatism. Certainly spiritual problems can be involved, and indeed mental ones too. Thus we see that once we allow Satan to get into us with his fear, he is free to afflict us in many ways.

We see the relationship between fear and cancer. Before modern treatments were discovered doctors preferred not to tell the patient that he or she had cancer, because that might have led them to become afraid of the cancer getting worse, and of it perhaps leading to death. It is known that if the person gives way to fear, the cancer actually grows more rapidly.

For many years doctors have been talking of treating 'the whole person'. They recognise that the attitude of mind of the patient has a definite effect on physical recovery. I ministered to a girl who had been anorexic. For weeks she had refused to eat more than one Mars bar a day, and then she switched to eating only one apple a day. The doctor thought she was unconscious when he said gravely to her parents, 'I don't think she can last the week out.'

The comment registered, however, in her mind and she resolved that she was not going to die. She recovered. The patient's attitude of mind has a bearing on the recovery of the body.

The connection between what a person believes and how their body functions is well illustrated in a book by an American doctor and a psychotherapist (*Getting Well Again* by Carl Simonton and Stephanie Matthews-Simonton). They record that in 1950 a new drug received sensational publicity in the United States as a 'cure' for cancer, and that it was being tested by the American Medical Association. A doctor who was involved in testing this drug had a patient with a generalised, far-advanced, malignancy involving the lymph nodes. The patient had huge tumour masses throughout his body and was in such a desperate physical condition that he frequently had to take oxygen by mask, and fluid had to be removed from his chest every two days.

When the patient discovered that his doctor was involved in research on the new drug, he begged to be given the new treatment. His doctor agreed and the patient's recovery was startling. Within a short time, the tumours had shrunk dramatically and the patient was able to resume a normal life, including flying his private plane.

Then, as reports of the negative results of the drug started being publicised, the patient took a dramatic turn for the worse. Thinking the circumstances extreme enough to justify unusual measures, the doctor told his patient that he had obtained a new super-refined double-strength version of the drug that would produce better results. In fact, the injections the doctor gave now were simply of sterile water. Yet the patient's recovery was even more remarkable. Once again, the tumour masses melted, the chest fluid vanished, and he was able to walk. He even went back to flying, and remained free of symptoms for over two months. His belief alone, independent of the value of the medication, had produced his recovery.

Then further stories appeared in the press. There were headlines that nationwide tests showed this drug to be useless in the treatment of cancer. Within a few days, the patient had died.

What we believe can affect how our bodies function. If a person's thoughts become dominated by fear, that, in turn, leads to tension and the normal recuperative processes of the body are weakened or checked. There are those in the medical profession who explain it thus: If you are under stress this will affect your limbic system. This in turn affects your hypothalamic system. The hormonal balance is then affected, and thus the immune system is suppressed.

In his excellent book on healing (*Healing at Any Price?*) Samuel Pfeifer writes that worry, anxiety and stress can disrupt the normal working of the autonomic nervous system.

If somebody comes to us then who, at root, is beset by fear, how do we help them? It is always much easier to pray *for* something, than to pray *against* something. The opposite of being fearful is to put our whole trust in Jesus and to receive His love and His peace.

We need therefore to help the person – or perhaps ourselves – to seek that lovely childlike trust in Him which the Lord looks for in those He loves so dearly. We can remember how much we hurt a fellow human being if they love us and we for our part refuse to trust them. We can recollect, therefore, that if we have refused to trust Jesus we have in fact been hurting Him. Surely we don't want that. Indeed we need to say sorry to Him for having hurt Him.

If we can allow the Lord to fill us with that childlike trust in Him, with His peace, and with His love, then it is not possible for us to be a prey to fear, nor to any of the problems which can follow. Then indeed we shall begin to receive the peace of God which passes our understanding.

Jesus knew how we needed to get rid of our worries. 'Cast all your anxiety on Him, because He cares for you,' Peter wrote (1 Pet 5.7). Jesus Himself said, 'Come to me, all you who are weary and burdened, and I will give you rest' (Mt 11.28).

However Satan will still try to infiltrate thoughts of fear into our minds. We need to train ourselves so that the moment we are aware of any feeling of fear we turn to Jesus and pray: 'Thank you Jesus that I am safe with you. Thank you that I know you will *always* look after me. Thank you Jesus that I can trust you in this situation too.' Trusting Jesus is not a matter of feelings but of decision.

Often we get people coming to us who say wearily and dispiritedly: 'I've been praying so long for such-and-such and the Lord doesn't seem to hear my prayer.' Often they will have been praying in desperation, perhaps thinking in their hearts, 'Lord, You can't have been listening when I prayed to You before. Lord, I'd better try again today, in the hope that perhaps this time You might actually listen.'

There is no power in that kind of prayer. If we have reached that point, we need to ask ourselves two simple questions:

1 Was the Lord listening when I asked Him for this before?
2 Was my prayer in line with His will?

If the answer to both those questions is yes – and usually it will be – then let us stop asking Him. Instead pray the prayer of faith which effectively says 'Lord, I am not going to ask You again because I know that You have heard. Because my prayer was in line with Your will I am thanking You now, in faith, that You have the answer to my prayer in hand.'

We can adapt this prayer if we have been plagued by fear or tension. 'Thank You, Lord,' we pray, 'that You are already answering my prayer and that You are already beginning to grow in me that childlike trust in You which I covet, and which You long so much for me to receive.'

That is the prayer of faith. The more we pray like that, thanking Him, the more we draw down His power to give us what we seek. We often tell people to pray that prayer of faith, many, many times during each day.

If Satan's favourite weapon is fear, I think guilt must be his next favourite. Samuel Pfeifer, head physician at a psychiatric clinic in Switzerland, says that a deep sense of guilt can impede the natural healing powers of the body in the same way that they are affected by tension and stress. Then, he says, 'all sorts of illnesses can arise' (*Healing at Any Price?* p. 31).

A professional psychiatrist who had become a Christian, and then been ordained, once said to Audrey and me, 'If we could only get it across to those who are in mental hospitals that the Lord forgives them for their sins, half the beds would be emptied overnight!' Humanly speaking, it does not come easily for us to accept the wonderful truth that Jesus does indeed forgive us our sins and washes us clean.

Jesus said to His followers, 'Whatever you loose on earth will be that which will have been loosed in heaven' (Mt 18.18, NIV alternative rendering). If someone comes to us who is burdened with their sins, and indeed with a guilt complex, we invite them to pray to Him, confessing all their sins, remembered or forgotten, and asking Him to forgive them. It is surprising how often they find it hard to think of anything specific for which to ask to be forgiven! In that case, we invite them to make a general confession of everything in them which is less than perfect.

Then if we feel that the repentance and the confession has genuinely been from the heart, I believe it is right to take the authority of Jesus and to say with absolute seriousness, 'As I stand here before God, I take the authority of Jesus, and I release you now in His Name from all the sins you have confessed.' We release the person in Jesus' Name. That does not mean, of course, that it is us who are forgiving their sins. It merely means that we are taking His authority and ministering forgiveness in His power and on His behalf. We often quote St John's words in the first chapter of his first letter, 'If we confess our sins, He is faithful and just, and will forgive us our sins and purify us from all unrighteousness' (1 Jn 1.9).

Sometimes we remind them of the passage in Isaiah, when he heard God declaring, 'I, even I, am He who blots out your transgressions and remembers your sins no more' (Is 43.25). I ministered to a girl who had sinned sexually. She had just accepted Jesus and when I pointed out that she had sinned, she prayed a lovely simple prayer of repentance, 'Jesus, I hadn't realised. I'm so sorry. I see it now as having been a sin. Will you please forgive me?' I told her that the Lord had now forgiven her, but to make the point clear I said, 'Do you realise that in the sight of God – which after all is all that matters – you are now once again a pure and undefiled virgin?' It took her a minute or two to take this in, but it helped her to see how fully the Lord forgives.

Sometimes when a person has confessed a particular sin we say, 'Supposing when you leave the mission you were to fall down our steps and break your neck so that you faced your Creator in the next world. Supposing you then said to Him, "Lord I'm so sorry for all those sins I was confessing earlier today", do you know what He would reply?'

Most people fall into the trap and say, 'He would tell me those sins were forgiven.' But this isn't what the Lord would say. He would look straight at the person and say, 'I don't know what you're talking about. I have no recollection of the sins you're referring to.'

The sin which is forgiven is the sin which is completely wiped out. It has become a non-event. God blots out our transgressions, and remembers our sins no more.

Nonetheless, we can be sure that Satan will try to bring back the previous feelings of guilt. We must help the person to see that the position is now different. We must help them to accept their forgiveness in faith based on the many verses in the Bible which assure us that the Lord forgives the sinner who repents.

Satan often works through echoes. We all know that if we are out walking in hilly country, we may give a shout and seconds later we will hear a voice calling back from the other side of the valley. It will only have been an echo.

Similarly, if Satan tries to put back on us the feelings of guilt, after we have confessed our sins to Jesus and have accepted His forgiveness by faith, then we can be sure that there is no power in those feelings. We can reject them robustly as being mere echoes.

The way to reject these echoes of guilt is by turning to Jesus and thanking Him for His forgiveness. Again we see that the prayer of thanks is a positive affirmation of biblical truth. The Lord's power is in this prayer of faith. Thus we learn to be victorious over that crippling feeling of guilt which Satan so often seeks to impose on us.

Another weapon which Satan often resorts to is the poor self-image. When I was growing up I suffered from self-consciousness and was unable to relate to others of my age. How I longed to be like my contemporaries. How I envied them when they were self-assured, amusing and popular. How I wished, quite simply, that I wasn't 'me'.

Many people have a poor self-image. If this is our problem, we need to remind ourselves that Jesus chose to make us as we are. If we keep saying, 'If only I were like them instead of like me', we are telling Jesus that He didn't know what He was doing and that we wish He had done a better job when He made us.

So often the person who has a poor self-image needs to look in the mirror and then to pray, 'Thank You, Jesus, that You made me just as I am, because You wanted me just as I am.' We can continue praying, 'Thank You, Jesus, that you love me as I am.' And then, 'Lord, I give myself to You, as I am.' We replace the negative thought with the positive prayer of thanks.

Jesus said that after loving God, the next most important thing in life was to love our neighbours as ourselves (Mk 12.31). For a long time I was mystified by what it meant to love myself. Surely it was an invitation for me to be introspective and self-centred?

But if I insist on always trying to give to my neighbour, and if I refuse to receive from my neighbour, the relationship becomes unbalanced. The situation becomes both frustrating and embarrassing for my neighbour. Moreover if I refuse to receive from him, I am denying him the pleasure of giving to me. Furthermore, I then make it impossible for him to love *his* neighbour – who in this case is me. In any healthy relationship between two people both have to be willing to give and to receive. Then a real friendship will develop.

A young man in his teens had been sent to an all-male boarding school. He wasn't happy there, he longed for the love of his home, and he sought loving relationships with those around him. He kept getting a 'crush' on this boy or that, and, when he left school, on this or that pretty girl, but he was always lonely. However, in time he began to see that if one is to form a stable relationship with another person one needs to rein in one's own emotional needs, and to allow the friendship to grow in a balanced way. I believe this is one aspect of what Jesus meant when He said, 'Love your neighbour as yourself.'

Forty years ago I was working on a tea plantation in Sri Lanka, staying with a couple in their forties. None of us were Christians then. The manager of the next-door plantation was in his forties and unmarried, and he was always doing things for other people. Somehow it was compulsive – he embarrassed us – and we used to joke about his 'doormat chivalry'. There needs to be a balance when it comes to giving and taking between our neighbour and ourselves.

I learnt more of what Jesus meant about loving oneself when I was ministering to someone who emphatically did not love herself; indeed she rejected herself. I realised that in this rejection lay the reason why she was unable to relate to other people. I told her that if Jesus loved her she had no right to reject herself. If He loved her, there was a sense in which she too must follow Him and love herself. I gave her the prayer, 'Jesus, thank You that You love me. Help me please, to join You in loving me.' As she continually prays that prayer, and as those words sink into her unconscious mind, she will come to accept herself. No longer will she be at war with herself, but she will receive the peace of God, and she will gain self-respect. Then she will come to find that she relates easily and naturally to other people.

So often it is the repeated prayer of thanks which releases the Lord's power to set us free and to heal us. If we send up an 'arrow' prayer of thanks roughly every ten minutes of our waking day, that adds up to about a hundred times a day, and we call it 'the hundred times prayer'. We don't need to wait until we feel like praying it. Pray it as an act of the will, and if possible aloud. To allow one second for it is enough. As we resolve to do this, we are carrying that 'Thank You' prayer all the while in our unconscious, accepting there the truth for which we are thanking Jesus. Moreover, in thanking Him we draw down His power.

Sometimes people come to us doubting some of the fundamental truths about the Christian faith. Perhaps they are doubting the love of Jesus. Perhaps they are doubting His ability to help them. Perhaps they are doubting His power.

Whether we allow ourselves to have doubts or not, is up to us. We can always replace a destructive habit of thought with a positive one. The way to deal with doubts is, as Paul wrote to the Corinthians, to 'take captive every thought' (2 Cor 10.5). Whenever we become aware of doubting, thank Jesus for the opposite – again perhaps a hundred times a day.

Suppose we have allowed ourselves to have doubts as to whether Jesus the man really was the Son of God. In that case, we need firmly to praise Him: 'Thank You, Jesus, that in truth You are the Son of God, and You always have been the Son of God.' If we doubt whether He really loves us, then we can keep praying, 'Thank You, Jesus, that You do love me.' If our doubt concerns what happened on the cross, we can then pray, 'Thank You, Jesus, that You set me free when You died for me on the cross.'

The way to deal with doubts is to affirm the truth as revealed in the Bible and to express that affirmation to Jesus as a prayer of grateful thanks.

As Basilea Schlink has written: 'God longs to do good things for us. But so few experience His goodness, because so few believe in it.'

7
Victory in Jesus

Almost every day we receive letters or telephone calls from people who want to give thanks to the Lord for answered prayer. Some forget. When Audrey and I were in Durham, a man said to me, 'A year ago, when you were here, your wife prayed for my wife. She had psoriasis on her hands which was causing great irritation. It went during the following couple of weeks and there has been no return since. I always meant to write and tell you, but somehow I never got round to it.'

When I went through our records of thanksgivings, I found that the most frequent healings were of cancer and depression. But we have seen many other illnesses healed, too.

In his book *Battered Bride*, David Winter, Head of BBC Religious Broadcasting, writes: 'There is no doubt that many people have received more effective help from spiritual healing than they have from psychiatry. I have myself met people who have been delivered from depression and anxiety: one person from a mental illness that had led to her being committed to Frampton Special Hospital. In her case it was the ministry of the

London Healing Mission that brought her to a psychological normality no-one could have predicted or expected, and her cure has now lasted several years.' Audrey and I remember praying for her. All we did was to lift her up to the healing love of Jesus.

We have seen depression healed quickly and slowly. The quickest was when a man in his fifties came to one of our services, having suffered with depression for many years. We prayed with him for ten minutes at the most, but he came back several months later to say that he had been instantaneously set free that evening.

Gradual healings of depression are, however, more common. There may be a physical cause of depression. A malfunctioning thyroid gland can contribute to depression. Similarly, it may be worth getting a packet of vitamin B6 pills from the chemist. Again it may help to go for a brisk walk every day.

Basically, depression comes from an emptiness in one's heart. That emptiness causes the person's thoughts to turn inwards. The more they allow this to happen, the heavier and the blacker becomes the cloud. The will becomes weaker. There is also much self-pity. 'You can never understand the utter hell which I'm enduring', is the kind of remark we hear.

It may be right for the person to receive anti-depressant pills for a time, but not in such strength as to sap the will-power even further. Those I have ministered to who have come through depression, have said that it was necessary to decide that they were going to come out of it.

The prospect of failure may hold a person back from taking this decision. This again is where the forgiveness of Jesus comes in. There is a sense in which every one of us is a failure. If we accept Jesus' own standard, when He said that we are to be perfect (Mt 5.48), we realise that all of us are failures.

There is however a lovely release in being able to turn to Him and acknowledge one's failure, in the prayer, 'Lord, You want me to be perfect,' (or, 'You want me to come out of this depression'), 'but, Lord, I can't do it. Nonetheless, if that is what You want me to do I accept that as my objective. But, Lord, You will have to help me.'

Each day we will feel that we have failed and have relapsed into the black self-pity of depression. It is vital, however, that we can then come back to Jesus, times without number, and say 'Lord, I'm sorry, I've let You down again.' Provided we are genuine in our desire to come through our difficulties with His help, we can always trust Him to reply, 'But I am longing to forgive this further failure and to wash you clean once more.' We may then feel that He is adding, 'Tomorrow morning you and I are going to start out again – together.' Such is the forgiveness of Jesus. Jesus told Peter that he was to forgive his brother seventy-seven times (Mt 18.22). We can interpret the thought as, 'You must forgive him, times without number.' If that was Jesus' instruction to a mere man, how much more will the same be true of Him.

If we can want to come out of the depression, if we can accept His help and His forgiveness whenever we fail and relapse back again into the blackness, then we can know that each time He will pick us up again. Each time we will have moved forward those few inches towards the time when we are finally free.

Having decided that our heartfelt desire is to come through it, we need to use our will to change the pattern of our thoughts. Our will by now will be weak and flabby and it is no use expecting it to function properly straight away. After all, if we go down with a bad bout of 'flu, our legs are wobbly when we first get up again. We need gradually to get the strength back into them by using them.

It is the same with the will. If we have been suffering, perhaps for years, from depression, we need to start using our will again and getting it to function properly. It is a gradual process. What matters is that we go on trying.

We need encouragement. Record every small victory in a notebook. It may simply be resisting the temptation to sit helplessly in front of the television, and going for a short walk. The following day we can record that we made it a longer walk and made ourselves walk faster. Maybe there are many household jobs we can't bring ourselves to do. Every bedroom drawer may need tidying out. Choose the smallest drawer and tidy that out. Then we can record another small victory.

As we continue to keep this record we see we are not quite such hopeless failures as we had thought. A pattern of 'winning' is beginning to emerge.

Often when we are ministering to the depressive they may reply, 'I wouldn't feel like doing what you are telling me to do.' We have to point out that their feelings don't matter. Those who just follow their feelings get deeper and deeper into depression. The way out of the mire is to set one's feet firmly on the Rock, which is Jesus. This is not easy – but Jesus never said it would be. But with His help we will gradually find that we are able to do it. 'I can do everything through Him who gives me strength', Paul wrote (Phil 4.13).

The depressive needs help to replace self-pity with

positive thoughts, and to pray, frequently, 'Lord, thank You that I can leave all my problems with You. Lord, I just want to love You, to trust You, and to lean on You.'

We need to resolve to turn our thoughts away from ourselves and towards Jesus, and towards other people. The best way to turn them to Jesus is to keep thanking Him, to thank Him non-stop for every blessing we can think of. The person who continually praises God cannot continue as a depressive.

The way to turn one's thoughts outwards to other people is to try not to be alone for too long, and when one is with others, to try deliberately to see things from their point of view and to think of what they are feeling and thinking. Changing the thought patterns is something we can't do on our own but, if we remember that the Lord is longing to be allowed to help us, then it is something which, with His help, we can achieve.

Builders' ladders used to be made of wood and were heavy. Two builder's labourers would walk along a pavement, each carrying one end of the ladder. It was no use one of them trying to carry the ladder by himself.

Similarly, it is no use our trying to tackle our problems ourselves, because we fail. It is no use, either, sitting back and leaving it to the Holy Spirit. He doesn't work that way. We need to picture ourselves picking up one end of the ladder while we thankfully accept His help on the other end. That way, we can move the ladder. That way, we can win over our problems. We do our bit and He is there helping us. Often we say to people, 'Learn to draw on the power of the Holy Spirit which you have within you.'

St Paul wrote, 'Thanks be to God. He gives us the victory through our Lord Jesus Christ' (1 Cor 15.57).

Many people who come here are negative or defeatist in their whole approach to life. One woman comes sometimes to our healing services, tells me her problems and within a few minutes she's bound to say, 'Of course, I'm such an old ditherer, aren't I?'

We are what we say. So long as she repeats these words, she continues, as it were, to pin that characteristic on herself. Surely the opposite of dithering is to enjoy the peace of God and to be strong in Him. If only she would thank Him then for His peace and His strength. Then as she thanked Him, she would draw down His strength to help her in her problems.

I like the story of the bishop who realised that he was a good deal more conscious than he should be when a pretty girl passed him on the pavement. He remembered that it is always easier to pray for something than to pray against something. He trained himself, whenever a pretty girl approached him on the pavement, to lift her up in prayer to Jesus. 'Lord, in Your love for that girl, You have given her good looks and beauty. Lord, strengthen her that she may not yield to temptation.'

Sometimes people come to us with marriage problems. Sadly, in our present culture, some of the basic truths about marriage are normally not taught. It is a fact that there are deep needs in the hearts of each one of us, man or woman, which can be met only in our one-to-one relationship of love with the Lord. St Augustine said, 'The human soul never finds peace until it finds God.' If only we can help people to find the satisfaction of their deepest desires in that perfect relationship of love with Jesus, they will be freed to love their partner in a new and deeper way.

Always, the Christian must put Jesus first, and then his or her partner. Paradoxically, the more each partner puts his or her relationship with Jesus first, the more they are set free to love each other. It is many years now since Audrey and I decided together that we were each going to put Jesus before the other – and how wonderfully since then He has deepened our love for each other.

If however two people marry who do not know the Lord, then they may find disappointment in marriage. One of them will begin to realise dimly that deep desires, which they had expected to be fulfilled in marriage, are not being met. Not knowing the Lord, they may turn to their partner with the words, 'I'm not finding myself fulfilled in you. You are not satisfying my emotional needs.'

Deep hurt is caused to the other person. Each begins to worry about the marriage. Then when an attractive person of the other sex comes along the thought will raise itself, 'If I were married to that person I wonder if I would find the fulfilment of all my needs?'

Thus many marriages drift towards breakdown because the people concerned have not been taught to find the satisfaction of their deepest needs in a relationship of love with the Lord.

Besides the need for a husband and wife to be friends together, there is always the need for the love which says, 'I'm married to so-and-so and I'm going to love them.' A marriage which is based on feelings alone is bound to be vulnerable, for feelings change. We need to base our lives on what the Bible teaches – then our feelings will come into line. There is so much talk today about a person's need for self-expression that we forget that our real fulfilment comes through unselfishness. In marriage we each need to decide to do something each day which will delight the heart of our partner. The real question in marriage is not, 'Have I married the right person', but, 'Am I being the perfect partner?'

We were asked to take a weekend on marriage in which three country parishes were joining. It occurred to us that, although we had thirty-five years of experience of marriage, we ought perhaps to read some of the theory as well; and we chose three good books on marriage.

Goodness knows how many married couples those three authors between them had counselled. They all said that however much a marriage seemed to have broken down, if each partner would simply resolve to love their partner, and themselves to be the perfect husband or wife, then in the course of time and against all expectation, firstly the friendship love would come back. Then, in due course, the fulness of the romantic love would come back, too.

When Disraeli, the great Victorian prime minister, was a young man, he used to frequent smart dinner parties. He once asked a duchess in her eighties at what age a woman ceased to feel passion. 'Young man', the elderly lady replied, 'if you want an answer to that question, you must ask an older woman than me.'

Every now and then, as we minister to people, the question of anger comes up. Is it right to be angry? Many people are puzzled about anger.

Psychiatrists voice the conventional wisdom of to-day. They warn of the dangers of bottling up anger, 'You must let your anger out!' they tell us. If we repress our anger and don't let it out, the anger isn't dealt with; it can remain festering deep within us.

But how are we to deal with it? If we go round venting our anger on other people we hurt them, and that cannot be within the will of a God of love. Indeed there is a subtle and refined form of selfishness which says: 'I've got to get rid of my anger and I don't care what effect it has on the person on whom I take it out.'

The other day we had someone at the mission who had been shattered by a Christian friend. 'You are not in the Lord's will,' she had shouted at her. 'You're not looking after your mother,' she accused her. 'And where is your duty to your husband?' she added. Subsequently the friend admitted: 'I was just getting rid of my anger' – not that the person who came to us had in any way been the cause of what had angered her!

Many people will point to the example of Jesus. 'Jesus was angry,' they will tell you. They point to the time when Jesus cleansed the Temple, casting out all those who were buying and selling goods and exchanging money. Often, however, they forget that this was no sudden outburst of rage on Jesus' part. We read that Jesus went to the Temple in the evening after His triumphal entry into Jerusalem and He had a good look round (Mk 11.11). But since it was already late he then went out to Bethany. It was the following day when He entered the Temple area and began driving out those who were buying and selling there. It is clear from the full account that this was no sudden outburst of temper but that Jesus looked round calmly at what He saw, and then went away and slept on it and, no doubt, prayed deeply through the situation. Then He went deliberately to the Temple to carry out what He saw needed to be done. Although the cleansing of the Temple is recorded in each of the four gospels, it is interesting that in none of the records are we told that Jesus was angry.

In the Sermon on the Mount Jesus quoted the old commandment from Exodus 20: 'Do not murder,' and

He went on: 'but I tell you that anyone who is angry with his brother will be subject to judgement' (Mt 5.22). James writes in his letter: 'Everyone should be quick to listen, slow to speak and slow to become angry' – while we read in Psalm 37: 'Refrain from anger and turn from wrath' (v8). Paul wrote: 'In your anger do not sin' (Eph 4.26). But he was quoting from Psalm 4 where the full passage reads: 'In your anger do not sin; when you are on your beds search your hearts and be silent'. Patience, gentleness and self-control are just as much part of the fruit of the Holy Spirit as love, joy and peace.

Are we beginning to reach the point where we find that psychiatry and the Bible are in conflict with each other over this question of anger? I think not. Sometimes when I am praying with someone who is beset by some physical affliction I find the anger rising in me. Am I angry with that person? Of course I am not. It is anger with Satan which I feel rising within me – anger that Satan should have dared to afflict a lovely Christian person with this particular sickness or infirmity.

The only time we are told in the gospel stories that Jesus was angry was when He healed the man with the shrivelled hand in the synagogue. We read: 'He looked round at them in anger and, deeply distressed at their stubborn hearts, said to the man: "Stretch out your hand"' (Mk 3.5).

We remember that Jesus, though always loving the sinner, hates the sin. Anger with Satan or with sin seems acceptable for the Christian.

But there are times when we are angry and it is not with Satan that we are angry. Anger can bubble up to the surface of our mind with seemingly irresistible force. We then have to decide whether we are going to explode into negative action, or whether we are going to turn to the Lord, perhaps screaming to Him in our pain, but in our screams seeking His appropriate action. God can then lead us into the particular action we should take so that the fire of the anger is consumed into a positive force for good. In that way none of the emotion is suppressed and we feel satisfied. Perhaps someone tells us that we can't do something. As we pray about this our anger turns into determination that, whatever anyone says, we are actually going to do what we have been told is beyond us!

There are other times when we simply have to recognise that to give way to the anger would be wrong. A man came to us whose wife was having to give up much of her weekends to look after her sick mother. As a result he felt his own weekends were being ruined. There was the temptation for him either to be angry with his mother-in-law or with his wife. Yet he realised that his mother-in-law couldn't help the fact that she was sick, while he had to admit that his wife was being a really loving daughter in the way she was looking after her. It would have been wrong for him to have given way to anger with either of them.

That man found the solution in turning to the Lord and praying through the situation with Him. Often we are angry because we have been hurt. We need to come to Him in prayer and open our hearts to Him. Then, as we pray through the hurt and as we come closer to the Lord in our relationship of love with Him, we will be able to let the anger go to Him. As we work at it and persist in seeking to draw closer and closer to Him in love, His peace will gently flow into our hearts and first the hurt, and then the anger, will gently be melted away. That way we are not repressing the anger. We are simply letting it go to Him. Often after we have prayed through such a situation with someone they have said, 'As you were praying, I actually felt something leave me.'

When we are angry with someone, the best thing we can do is to pray for them. It helps them – and it helps us too. 'Pray for them that persecute you,' Jesus said (Mt 5.44).

Audrey and I were having lunch with Colin and Caroline Urquhart. Colin told us that he had been studying the Bible afresh and he saw how, all through it, God was looking for faith in His people. Indeed we learn from the letter to the Hebrews that 'without faith it is impossible to please God' (Heb 11.6). We can, I believe, build up our faith by that repeated and affirmative prayer of thanks, 'Thank you, Lord, that You have the answer to my prayer in hand even now.' But so often, we have difficulty in even starting to have faith.

We can derive much comfort then from the experience of the father with the epileptic boy. When Jesus came down from the Mountain of Transfiguration with Peter, James and John, a crowd ran towards Him. There was a man in the crowd whose son had an unclean spirit which made him dumb, often hurling him to the ground, and often, too, throwing him into fire or water to kill him. The man spoke to Jesus, 'If you can do anything, take pity on us and help us.'

'If you can?' said Jesus, 'Everything is possible for him who believes.' Then we have the father's classic reply, 'Lord, I believe. Help Thou my unbelief' (Mk 9.24, AV). Or, as we read in the NIV, 'I do believe. Help me overcome my unbelief!'

How many of us are in the position of that father, longing to be able to believe and yet conscious of the unbelief which is in us? Like that father, we can turn to Jesus, telling Him of our desire to believe, and seeking His help for us to be able to overcome the unbelief.

The point of the story is that the man's desire to believe was enough. Jesus went ahead, set his son free and healed him.

What comfort there is in knowing that, provided we want to believe, then the Lord will overlook the unbelief in us. That desire to believe releases the Lord's healing power as it did two thousand years ago.

Often we can help to build up a person's faith if we remind them of three 'given facts' which are always true, whoever we are and whatever we are praying for.

The first is that the Lord loves us with a perfect love. If He is perfect Himself, then His love for us must be perfect. I have been fortunate in having grown up in a loving family and then having a wonderfully loving wife and children. But I need to remember that the love of the Lord for me is far more wonderful than the love of any of my family. The Lord loves us on the inside. He sees into our very hearts.

The second given fact is that, because of His perfect love for us, He always wants to do what is perfect in us. We are always ready to compromise and to settle for what is second best. This is never the case, though, with the Lord. Since He is perfect, He always desires what is perfect for those He loves with such a wonderful love.

The third given fact is that, because of that enormous once-and-for-all victory which Jesus won for our sakes on the cross, He has the power to give us what is perfect for us.

As we reflect on these three given facts, they help us to have more faith.

8

Prayers which are Answered

As we minister to someone we need to lay our human emotions on one side. It often amazes me when I find, as I pray with someone, that I am loving them with the selfless love of Jesus, even if they might be humanly unattractive.

When we pray with someone, we always stand up. I stand on the left-hand side of the person I am praying for. I often explain that I am not standing in front because I want them to see Jesus in front of them. In addition, there are times when someone may fall under the power of the Holy Spirit (*cf* Jn 18.6) and if one is standing at their side it is easier to step round, slip a hand under each of their armpits and lower them gently to the ground.

We pray with our eyes open. One can tell so much from the body language of the person one is praying for. One may see the quick fluttering of the eyelids which so often indicates that the Holy Spirit is falling in power upon the person. One may see the relaxing of the shoulders as the person begins to receive the peace of God. The hands held out and with the palms upwards, may have begun by being tense, but one watches them relaxing. Sometimes one sees a gentle quivering. Indeed, at times, one sees the person reaching out physically to Jesus. It is worth watching, too, for that slight rhythmic swaying of the body which again may indicate the power of the Holy Spirit coming upon them.

Sometimes that swaying may go further and they fall gently backwards under the power of the Holy Spirit. God is sovereign and He is not to be tied down by man-made rules. We have seen people obviously receiving the power of the Holy Spirit as they remained standing. Equally, we have sometimes wondered whether there hasn't been an extra release on the person's part as he or she puts all their trust in Jesus and allows themselves to go over backwards.

Yet at large healing meetings, where everyone seems to fall backwards as soon as someone lays hands on them, there can be an element of auto-suggestion. I remember a lovely Christian speaker at one of our annual conferences. Everyone, including myself, queued for him to pray for them. Virtually everyone fell backwards. Yet two days later, when I gave people the opportunity to testify to what the Lord had done for them at the conference, though fifty people came forward to testify, not one of them referred to anything the Lord had done through that man's ministry.

Sometimes I have tried in my own mind to formulate a rule: 'If I do it this way, the Holy Spirit responds like that. If I do that, He then responds in such and such a way.' But each time we are brought back to the realisation that God is sovereign. The following day He works in a different way and I am back to square one. Let us always remember that God is not to be manipulated. We are simply to love him and follow Him and pray in line with His directions.

As we pray with people we are helping them to open their hearts to receive the love of Jesus, and then to pour out their own hearts to Him in return. We may use the picture of their opening the windows of their heart to let in the sunshine of His love. We may use the simile of basking in the warm sun on a summer's day. We may indeed tell the person to picture themselves being like a beautiful flower in a summer garden. Drinking in the life-giving light of the Lord is a necessary part of prayer.

One of the difficulties is that all of us have been hurt emotionally during our lives. Instinctively, we then put up barriers to protect ourselves against being hurt again. But those barriers are not selective. They keep out pain but they also keep out love. We need to help the person to become vulnerable once again. We need to help them to lower the barriers, and to allow the love of Jesus to come flowing in. They may wonder what would happen if again they were hurt emotionally. In reply we may tell them that the real defence against being hurt is to live in a strong relationship of love with the Lord. Then if they are hurt by others they will be able to hand the hurt over to Jesus. That way, He is able to set us free without our putting up new barriers.

Meanwhile how do we pray with people? God is not glorified by wishy-washy prayers. I don't believe He is glorified by the prayer which finishes with the escape clause 'if it be Thy will'. We need to bring our wills into play but always remembering that our wills need to be perfectly aligned with His will. Some people pray, for example, 'Lord, heal them *in accordance* with Your Will'.

Often in prayer we need to be resolute. We have no record of Jesus instructing His disciples to pray for the sick. His recorded words to them were, 'Go and heal them!' (*eg* Mt 10.8). It takes courage to pray with the prayer of command, but there are times when we should.

We read that Jesus 'rebuked the fever' in Peter's mother-in-law (Lk 4.39). Often with cancer, for example, we find ourselves rebuking in prayer the darkness of the cancer in the person's body. Often we tell it that it has no place in the body of a Christian person. Normally we will take the authority of Jesus and instruct it to be gone. Often then it seems right to see the healing light of Jesus flowing into the afflicted part of the person's body and to praise Him for His healing power flowing into them.

We may need to pray specifically. Pastor Cho in South Korea, has much to say about that. When he was very poor, he lived in one tiny room. 'I ate on the floor, I slept on the floor and I studied on the floor, because I was too poor to buy any furniture'. He asked the Lord to provide some furniture and month after month there was no answer to his prayer. Eventually, he remonstrated and prayed, 'Lord, why are You not answering my prayer?'

He felt the Lord replied that he was not asking precisely enough. His request for 'furniture' could cover so many different things. He tells how he responded by giving a precise list of the furniture he would like from God. He asked for an executive's desk made of the finest Philippine teak, a business executive's chair on swivels, and, for good measure, a bicycle with shiny handlebars and three-speed gears, to help him visit his flock in their homes.

Pastor Cho must always have been a remarkable man. He was thrilled at having, he believed, found how to pray in such a way that the prayer would be answered. The following Sunday, he called all his congregation to rejoice with him that God had indeed given him the business executive's desk, the chair and the bicycle. Two or three young men in his congregation came up to rejoice with him afterwards. 'Pastor, may we come to your home and see these things the Lord has so wonderfully provided for you?' they asked. 'But of course', he replied, and he led them to the door of his tiny room.

He took out his key and opened the door. The room was empty. 'But where are these things that God has given you, Pastor?' the young men asked.

'Well, where were you,' Cho replied, 'before you were born? You were in your mother's tummy, weren't you? All these things which I asked for are coming, but just for the moment, you've got to accept that I am pregnant with them.'

The word spread like wildfire through his congregation that Pastor was now pregnant with a business executive's desk, an executive chair and a bicycle. But the last laugh was on Pastor Cho, for quite soon after Cho's specific prayer to God, God gave him precisely the items of furniture he had asked for.

We need to be completely surrendered to the will of God. A book called *Miracle in the Mirror* recounts how a girl in Sri Lanka fell downstairs, injured herself, and in due course became totally paralysed. She was unable to do anything, lying helplessly upon her back in hospital.

For a long time she would joke with her friends when they came to visit her, looking forward to when the Lord would have healed her and they would be able to enjoy themselves together again. But the Lord didn't

heal her. Eventually, her spirit broke and she contem-
plated the prospect that she might be left lying there,
helpless for the rest of her mortal life. She prayed
robustly, 'Lord, if that really is Your will, then I will
continue to praise You.' For some days she prayed that
prayer of total surrender to the will of God. Then He
acted, and one afternoon she got up and dressed,
completely healed.

As I understand that story, the girl had a strong
character, and perhaps unconsciously, was almost willing her healing. It seems that it was only when she laid
aside her will and promised to praise God whatever
happened that His power to heal her was released.

Merlin Carothers tells a similar story concerning a
father and his daughter, who was very badly injured in
a car accident. After several months the medical prognosis was that she would never have the normal use of
her brain again. For years her father travelled the
twenty miles from his home to the hospital. Each time
when he entered her ward he would find her sitting
upright in bed staring blankly at the wall in front of her.
Even when he spoke to her or touched her, she gave no
sign of recognition.

Then one day, as he set out for the hospital, it seemed
as though he heard a voice within him saying, 'I want
you to thank me for your daughter's condition.' He
ignored the voice. The idea of giving thanks for what
appeared to be the wrecking of his child's life was
preposterous. But as he continued to drive towards the
hospital, the voice seemed to repeat, 'I want you to
thank me for your daughter's condition.' At that, he lost
his temper. 'If that's you speaking, God,' he said, 'I
think you're doing a rotten job. You're meant to be
healing her and you're doing nothing about it. And the

last thing I'm going to do is to thank you for her being the way she is!'

Nonetheless, the voice seemed gently to persist, and, as he was going up to his daughter's ward, he prayed with the utmost reluctance under his breath, 'Lord, in sheer obedience to You, and for no other reason, and with the heaviest of hearts, I'm going to praise You. I'm going to thank You for my daughter's condition.'

A few moments later, as he entered the ward, his daughter looked up and called out, 'Daddy!' Three months later she was back home.

Again, this story seems to emphasise the need for our complete surrender to the will of God. It is no use willing God to do something. He is sovereign, and He is not to be manipulated by us. In the same way, it is no use our getting angry with Him. What He requires of us is our complete submission to His sovereign will.

At first sight, there appears to be a contradiction between the submission which He looks for in us, and Cho's lesson that we need to be bold and pray specifically. I believe, however, that the two lessons are complementary rather than contradictory. We need to be completely submissive to His will, and then to step out in faith, praying resolutely for what we believe He is asking us to pray for.

Often, He wants us to hand our problem over to Him – and not to take it back again! When, Colin Urquhart's son was a little boy, he suffered badly from eczema. Colin felt the Lord telling him that he would be healed but not until he was fourteen (which is what actually happened). As the little boy grew up there were many kindly adults who would sympathise with him over his eczema. Invariably he would look up at the grown-up and, as he shrugged his shoulders, he would say,

'Eczema? It's not my problem, it's Jesus'.' If only we could all achieve the spiritual maturity of that little boy!

But if something really is troubling us, how is it possible for us firstly to hand it over to Jesus, and then, perhaps even more important, to ensure that we do not take the problem back again? We need first to remember the power of the spoken word. Paul wrote about the Sword of the Holy Spirit which is the Word of God. Isaiah heard God say, 'My word will not return to me empty but will accomplish what I desire' (Is 55.11). The whole of creation came into being through the spoken word of God (Gen 1). Similarly, we ourselves need to speak forth the word, 'Jesus, I've asked you to intervene in this situation. I believe my prayer was in line with your will. Therefore I'm now going to leave the problem in your hands, acknowledging in faith that henceforth it is your problem and no longer mine.'

Then, as so often, we need to seal our prayer with thanks: 'Thank you, Jesus, that you are now acting on that problem. Thank you, Jesus, that it is your problem. Thank you, Jesus, that I can leave it all to you. Thank you, Jesus, that I'm free from all worry and all concern about it, because you are almighty and you have the answer in your hands. Thank you, Lord.'

Very likely we shall try and start worrying about it again. After all, by now, we will have got into a bad thought pattern and our unconscious will continually be feeding the worrying thoughts to us. But each time we need to turn resolutely to Jesus and reaffirm what we have done, 'Thank you, Jesus, that this is no longer my problem. Thank you, Jesus, that I am at peace now because I have left it in your hands and you are working on it. Thank you, Lord.' The prayer of thanks which is

prayed in faith and continuously, does indeed set the
seal on the Lord's answer to our prayer.

We recently had an example of the power of the word
spoken in prayer. C's daughter had had glandular fever
and the doctor had said that it would be a year before
she would be really fit again. C is a lovely Christian
woman and she came up from Gloucestershire to see
Daphne, who is one of the team here. Daphne knew
what to do. She took the sword of the Holy Spirit (Eph
6.17) and she cut the child free from the negative words
which had been spoken by that doctor.

There was no question of blaming the doctor. He had
acted for the best according to his medical knowledge;
but Daphne had superior knowledge. She cut the child
free from the effect of those words. Within a fortnight
the child was perfectly fit again. It is possible for
negative words, however well intentioned by the person
who speaks them, to have something like the power of a
curse.

Sometimes when I am praying I stop and ask myself
who I am actually praying to. Jesus said to His disciples, 'When you pray, say "Our Father in Heaven"'
(Mt 6.9). If we just address Him as 'God', we are not
being very specific, but if we pray to 'our Heavenly
Father', not only are we being more precise but we can't
fail to be right, because that is what Jesus told us to do.

Yet, we need to remember that the power is in the
name of Jesus. If one seeks to draw fully on the power of
the risen Lord, whether it be in deliverance, or in
spiritual warfare in other areas, we know from experience that the power is in His name. That this would be
so was revealed by Jesus Himself when He spoke to His
disciples only minutes before being taken from their
sight and ascending into Heaven. 'All authority in

heaven and on earth has been given to me!' He proclaimed (Mt 28.18).

As I read those words, I am filled with wonder. There was Jesus, having completed His ministry, having been crucified, risen from the dead, and about to sit for ever in Heaven at the right hand of God the Father, and He was saying that someone had given Him something more! Who could have given Him anything, let alone such sweeping authority? The answer can clearly only point us to God the Father.

In Old Testament times, the Jews knew the personal Name of God. From about 400 BC, that Name was not used. The Jews stood in such awe of the power which they knew flowed from the use of that Name that they dared not mention it. The personal Name of God was finally lost at the fall of Jerusalem in AD 70.

Sometimes I have asked myself why, in His sovereign will, God did not choose to reveal once again His personal Name, with all the glory and the power which would be released by the use of that Name. The answer, however, seems clear. There was no need for Him to reveal that Name again, for He had put all authority in Heaven and earth into the Name of Jesus.

Because of these two truths – Jesus' instruction that we should pray to our Heavenly Father, and the placing of all power in the name of Jesus – many prayers are directed to God the Father and are submitted to Him in Jesus' name. Sadly, however, in many cases, this form of prayer has just become a religious formula. We need to realise that, in Jesus' own words, the power is indeed in His name.

The New Testament epistles bear out the authority which is in the name of Jesus. Moreover, in Acts, invariably that early church used the name of Jesus.

When the crippled beggar looked to Peter and John as they were going to the temple to pray, Peter replied, 'Silver or gold I do not have, but what I have I give you. In the name of Jesus Christ of Nazareth, walk!' (Ac 3.6). That early church needed spiritual power to survive and to grow in the face of often intense opposition. Christians knew that the power was in the name of Jesus.

We read in Corinthians how the end will come. Jesus will hand over the Kingdom to God the Father, after He has destroyed all dominion, authority and power, 'For He must reign until God has put all His enemies under His feet' (1 Cor 15.25). When He has done this, the Son Himself will be made subject to Him who put everything under Him, 'so that God may be all in all' (1 Cor 15.28). Thus we get a glimpse of the relationship between God the Father and God the Son.

For a long time I was baffled by the historic definition of the Trinity: 'Three persons in one person; one person in three.' Yet if we remember that each of them – Father, Son and Holy Spirit – is absolutely perfect we begin to see the unity between them, for all three of them are identical in perfection. Often with identical twins we will notice the unusual affinity between them. Yet although they started as one, they went on to develop as separate individuals. If we remember that each of the three persons of the Trinity is perfect in love, in holiness, and in majesty we can begin to perceive their 'one-ness'. Thus, Jesus said: 'I and the Father are one' (Jn 10.30).

In all prayer, we are to worship Him and glorify Him, for the Lord indeed inhabits the praises of His people. We often find that it is as we join together in praise and worship that His power to heal is released upon us. I once led some two hundred people in praise and prayer in a church in the City. We were aware of the power of the Holy Spirit falling upon us and I noticed one woman upon whom this power seemed particularly to be falling. She told me afterwards, 'I was healed while you were praying for us all.' 'Of what?' I asked. 'Of cancer in my chest,' she replied. Obviously there was no medical certificate at that stage. Clearly no doctor had seen her during the few moments since we had finished praying. Often people know within themselves that they have been healed.

The Lord may choose to heal in different ways. It is not for us to try to tell Him how He is to perform His wonderful healing work. There may be the instantaneous healing, which the world calls a miracle; there may be a delayed healing; often there is a gradual healing. Quite often, the trouble may actually get worse for days or even weeks before it begins to clear up. How He heals is His business and not ours.

I am not aware of the Lord ever having performed two miracles for the same person during our ministry. Indeed, almost invariably, when there has been an instantaneous healing, the Lord will leave something else wrong which requires a real effort on the part of the person before it can be put right. I think of a woman in her late thirties who came here suffering from epilepsy, asthma and bronchitis. As we prayed for her, she fell under the power of the Holy Spirit. There were several characteristic outbursts of coughing and it seemed as though some unclean things had left her. We learned afterwards that the sicknesses had gone. She had been on a high dosage of drugs to counter the epileptic fits, and yet she was, nonetheless, still having two or three fits a week. After that time of ministry, she had no more

epileptic fits, nor did she have another attack of asthma
or bronchitis.

But she was left with a cruel family situation. She had
had to divorce her husband years before. She had spoilt
her children, who were now in their teens, and they
were behaving abominably to her. Having been much
rejected in her own childhood, she was finding it
terribly hard to cope with her children's behaviour.

It would, of course, have been quite possible for the
Lord to have brought about some instantaneous healing of the situation, but He left her with it. Where
relationships were involved she needed to grow the
hard way. After several years they were beginning to
come right, but during that time she had learnt much
and her faith had grown. Much as we would like
everything to be done the easy way, that is not necessarily the Lord's way. He will never 'spoon-feed' us. He
wants what is perfect for us and, in pursuit of that
objective, He may well discipline us (Heb 12.6ff).

We see how nature works through giving a stimulus.
Grass-eating animals have to travel quite long distances, foraging for their food. Flesh-eating animals
have to run fast and hard to catch their prey. The
exercise keeps them in the peak of condition. An eagle
will make its nest from twigs. The hen bird lays her eggs
and begins to rear the young chicks when they hatch
out. But, once they have grown sufficiently for their
wings to support them, the hen bird encourages her
chicks to launch out and fly by gradually dismantling
the nest. Time and again in the world of nature, we see a
stimulus being applied for the good of the animal or
bird concerned.

Since God is the God of all creation, we can learn
much about Him from the world of nature. I believe

that He will always seek to stimulate us to reach out for more and more of His love and His strength. It would not be good for us if He just did everything without our ever having to exert ourselves.

Audrey prayed for a nurse in Salisbury and we both learnt much from the outcome. The nurse's problem was that she had cancer of the breast. Audrey was alone with her at the time and she asked Audrey to feel the hard lump in her breast. They then prayed together and at the end Audrey, who is a cautious person, said, 'I believe the Lord has healed you'. The nurse said, 'I think so too'.

We heard nothing more for three months, when the nurse 'phoned Audrey to tell her the story. For four weeks after Audrey prayed with her, the lump actually got bigger. Was she therefore going to follow what common sense indicated and say to herself, 'The Lord may heal other people, but from the fact that my growth has continued to get bigger, it is obvious that He's not going to heal me'? If she had followed that course, she would have gone to the hospital without delay to have the growth cut out.

Or was she going to pray: 'Lord, I don't mind about this silly lump on my breast. I believe that when Audrey prayed with me, You did heal it and I'm just going to go on thanking You that Your healing process has already begun and that You are going to heal this lump completely.'

She chose the second course. For four weeks she praised the Lord that, against all the evidence, He was healing her of the cancer. At the end of the four weeks the lump started to go. When it had gone completely, she went to the hospital, had all the tests and was told that there was no cancer anywhere in her body.

As I reflected on that experience, I found myself
praying: 'Lord, wouldn't it have been kinder on Your
part if, since You wanted to heal her anyhow, You'd
done it straight away instead of stringing her along for
those four long weeks?' It seemed that the reply He gave
was along these lines, 'I loved her too much to do that.'

I came to see that the Lord in His kindness and love
had actually done two things for that nurse, instead of
the one action of instantaneous healing. In addition to
healing the cancer, He enabled her to grow much
stronger in faith as she held on through all that long
testing time. He finished by doing more for her than she
had asked for. She was never the same again, either
physically or spiritually.

We attended a healing conference given by Francis
McNutt, who has written *Healing* and *The Power to Heal*
and who has been active in the healing ministry since
the 1960s. He said that in his experience there were
probably twenty-five instances of people receiving par-
tial or delayed healing for every one instance where
there was an instantaneous healing. He stressed the
relationship between the amount of time and effort that
was invested in the prayer for healing and the amount
of healing which resulted.

I realised that as we send people away after prayer,
urging them to keep thanking and praising Jesus, we
are inviting them to soak themselves in prayer in the
way that Francis meant. We realised that his experience was the same as ours. We too see many more cases
of gradual or delayed healing than of instantaneous
healing. The underlying reason would be the same.
Jesus wants to draw us closer to Him, and He wants us
to press onwards, seeking Him in prayer so that we may
grow spiritually as well as being healed.

Sometimes I tell people, 'You won't get magic if you come here.' I explain that there are instantaneous healings, but that often the Lord in His mercy chooses to heal gradually so that He may 'grow' the person spiritually as well as healing them.

This is not, however, the pattern described in the Gospels, where Jesus almost always healed instantaneously. There was the one recorded occasion when He Himself had to pray twice before a blind man could see perfectly (Mk 8.23–25), but the general pattern seems to have been one of instantaneous healing.

Yet we read in Hebrews that 'Jesus Christ is the same yesterday, and today, and for ever' (Heb 13.8). Has Jesus changed after all? What is the explanation for what appears to be a different pattern in His healing today?

I believe the answer lies in the sheer personality of Jesus. Think of those many occasions when hundreds of peasants trudged for mile after mile under the blazing sun to be with Jesus out in the wilderness. We realise something of the sheer personality Jesus must have had. People just loved being with him. Those peasants were not 'religious' people. Yet they walked long distances, often forgetting their bodily needs, apparently not giving a thought about their return home, simply to be with Jesus. They must have had great faith in Him.

The experience would have been unforgettable. First one person, then another was brought up to Jesus – and was healed! One can imagine how the enthusiasm spread through that crowd. They must have poured out their hearts in wonder and admiration – and in worship – as they saw one sick person after another set free and healed by this wonderful young teacher from Galilee.

They would always have remembered their day with Jesus. In those few hours together they would have had the opportunity to enter into the kind of living relationship with Him into which He is always seeking to draw us. Having entered into that living relationship on that one occasion, the Lord was free to release the physical healing instantaneously.

Jesus Christ is certainly the same yesterday, today and forever. The conditions today however are different from those of two thousand years ago. He always does what is best for us under the conditions of the time.

As one prays, one must always be listening with that 'third ear'. Audrey and I were conducting a healing service in a small town near Oxford. A woman told me afterwards that she had just been diagnosed as having cancer, and would I please pray for her? The obvious answer seemed to be, 'Yes, of course.' But as I collected my thoughts and sought to enter into the peace of Jesus, prior to praying, I found that no words were there. The Holy Spirit simply wasn't leading me in prayer.

It flashed through my mind that either the Holy Spirit was thinking of something else, or I was not meant to be praying. I then realised what He was saying. 'I'm not going to pray for you,' I said to the woman, 'because there is no cancer left for you to be healed from. The Lord has already answered your prayer.' I urged her, however, to keep thanking Him continually that He had, in fact, already healed the cancer and I reminded her that it is in thanking Him that we actually draw down His power.

A year later the woman wrote to me. She had continued to see her specialist every three months. At each of the next two visits, her specialist had told her that the cancer had got no worse. At the third visit, that is nine months after she and I had prayed together, he said, 'If I didn't know you had cancer I wouldn't have said that you had it.' When she saw him a year after we had prayed together, apparently her specialist had shrugged his shoulders and said, quite simply, 'You just do not have any cancer.'

Twelve months later, she wrote again, having finally been discharged by her specialist: 'I saw him last week and he said, "As far as I can see, you are completely cured and you need never see me again!" When I thanked him, he said, "I have done *nothing*. I cannot understand it. What is your secret?" I told him it was faith in God, at which he said, "How I wish I could pass on your remedy to my other patients."'

It is certain that, just as it is in the nature of the Lord to love, to comfort, to heal, and to make whole, so it is in the nature of the opposition – whether you call him Satan, the devil or the enemy – to drag down, to ensnare, to damage, and eventually to destroy. After a prayer for healing, Satan will always try to steal our healing from us. He will attempt to insinuate doubts and thus get between us and Jesus. If he can destroy our trust in Jesus, then he has broken the two-way flow of love between us and the Lord, and the power to heal will be interrupted.

It is always essential after prayer for healing to keep on thanking the Lord robustly and in faith for His answer. Each of these little prayers of thanks is an affirmation of faith, and Jesus was always looking for faith in those to whom He ministered. In thanking Him in faith we draw down His power to help us.

We can go further. We can set aside three times in the day when we spend five minutes picturing little tongues of fire flickering over the parts of our body which need healing. We can picture ourselves healed and well again. This will often help us, as we continue to thank Jesus that He is in fact healing us. If we do this for longer than five minutes at a time, we may get tired. Stick to a routine, doing it at set times.

You may say, 'I cannot sincerely thank the Lord for His healing if I don't feel it.' This is just where faith comes in. We need to speak out in faith, regardless of our feelings (or lack of them). Thank the Lord for what, in His mercy and kindness, we trust Him to be doing for us.

Some people teach that we should thank the Lord that we are healed even when there is no sign of any change. I do not have the faith to do this, but I can quite readily pray: 'Thank You, Lord, that You've heard our prayer. Thank You that You have got this person's healing in hand.' I cannot in all sincerity thank the Lord that black is white, when I see that it is still black. I can, however, thank Him that He already has in hand the process by which black will indeed be changed to white.

Moreover, let us never try to limit God in the way we expect Him to answer prayer. He is the God of all creation. He invented the laws of nature and of medicine just as He invented the laws of prayer. He may answer our prayer for healing through doctors or nurses, or He may answer through the power of the Spirit released in prayer. It is not for us to tell Him how to answer prayer. Indeed we can see some of the different ways in which the healing power of Jesus works, and we remember John's words that, 'without Him nothing was made that has been made' (Jn 1.3).

When we first bought a little house in the country we found some apple trees in the garden. One tree had been cut straight across some three feet above the ground. There was just an extended stump. As the years went by, we saw, first, a small twig growing upwards from the stump. Then gradually the stem of that twig grew and expanded. Before we left that house the new stem had grown to completely envelope the whole stump and one could not tell that the tree had ever been cut across. The tree was restored to its original beauty with branches, foliage, and indeed fruit. The original perfection was restored without the intervention of man, and through God's own natural laws.

Consider a person who breaks an arm. He is taken to hospital and the surgeon employs all his medical skill to set the fractured bones in their right relationship, one to the other. But the surgeon cannot heal the fracture. Having set the bones, he then leaves the consolidation of the fractured bone, as it comes together again in one mended bone, to the power of nature. Here we see God working both through the medical skill of the surgeon and through the laws of nature. The skill of the medical profession involves the doctor or the nurse stimulating the natural recuperative powers of the human body.

We are always glad to work with the medical profession, and we welcome the many instances of the Lord healing through a combination of the natural power He has ordained, the laws of medicine which He has decreed, and His spiritual power released in prayer.

9
Healing – Memories and Homosexuals

Sometimes people come to us and say, 'I have come for healing of my memories.' We gently tell them that it is not within our power, nor indeed within the power of anyone else, to heal the deep emotional hurts which many people have suffered. We can only seek to help the person to open their heart to the healing power of the Holy Spirit, and to invite Him to come in and do the healing. Sometimes, He may even heal despite our efforts!

I ministered to a woman who since childhood had feared the dark. Her childhood home had had no indoor sanitation, only an earth closet outside, and she remembered all too keenly her fear of going out into the dark to find her way to the unlit loo.

As we prayed, it seemed that her memory of that fear needed to be healed. As I understand it, one helps the person to relive the episode which is still hurting them, only this time in the presence of Jesus, so that His healing can be introduced into the situation. Often one can help a person to recall a situation more vividly if they can remember some of the colours.

We pictured together the kitchen with the back door leading to the loo. I asked her the colour of the linoleum and the walls. We remembered the sensation of her wanting to go outside, but before she moved over to open the door, we called to mind the presence of Jesus who, as she now realised, had been with her all the time. As we prayed together, she reached out and held Jesus' hand. Holding His hand, the fear began to go and she began to feel safe with Him. We then pictured her moving forward, opening the door for Jesus, and beckoning Him as He still held her hand, to come through with her.

My thought had been to help her to experience, once more, the fear of the dark, once she got outside, and then for that fear to be dispelled as she recollected that she was still holding Jesus' hand and that with Him there can be no fear. I tried describing the scene to her as she moved out through the door. 'Jesus is moving through the door with you now. You are still holding onto His hand, you are still feeling the comfort of His presence and His love. Now He is shutting the door behind you. You move out of the light of the kitchen windows and you and Jesus together are moving out to where it is quite dark.'

'Oh, no we're not!' she cried, 'It's brilliantly light!' I tried to reason with her, as my ideas were being completely upset by her insistence that there was no darkness.

Then I realised where I had been mistaken. Jesus is light (Jn 8.12). With Him there can be no darkness. The Holy Spirit in His wisdom had overruled me. Once she accepted that Jesus had been with her all the time, His presence dispelled the darkness, and with it the fear which had troubled her for so long. It seemed that the

Holy Spirit in His gracious love was covering up for my mistake!

On another occasion, while I was praying for a man in his forties, I had a picture which I could not get out of my mind. I interrupted my praying and shared the picture with him. Within two minutes he had collapsed in a heap on the floor, under the power of the Holy Spirit. Subsequently he told me that the picture had brought back to his mind the occasion when he was quite a small boy, when he had realised that he could never again rely on his mother. At the time he had been unable to handle this experience and, as so many of us do, he had pushed it down into his unconscious.

When we do that, however, a painful memory is not healed. It remains there festering. On this occasion the Lord in His mercy used the picture He had given me to bring the memory back to his consciousness. He then healed it under the power of the Holy Spirit.

Sometimes people have great difficulty forgiving those who have hurt them. Yet to forgive is necessary. Jesus said, 'When you pray, forgive if you have anything against anyone.' I ministered to a woman in her forties who was damaged emotionally by her father in childhood. There was no physical abuse but her father had never wanted a daughter and he couldn't stand the thought that she was a girl. She avoided him whenever she could, but she couldn't avoid him at mealtimes. The memory which tormented her still was of her father sitting at the end of the table and continually making sarcastic and wounding remarks about her. This went on for as long as she was growing up and had prevented her from forming a stable relationship with a man.

It was fairly easy to point to the need for her to forgive her father. She spoke the words of forgiveness as the two of us prayed together. But how was she to forgive her father from her heart? The feelings of our unconscious, deeply stored, are beyond the control of our human wills.

While we were praying we sought to relive the repeated experience of her suffering in that dining room. I asked her the colour of the carpet and the wallpaper. But then she took over. 'As I sit there I can feel Jesus standing behind me,' she said. 'I can feel His hands on my shoulders, and I can actually feel His power flowing into me. I want to say something to my father,' she added.

Then I heard these lovely words of forgiveness, 'Daddy, I'm so sorry. Daddy, I just wanted you to be happy. I'm so sorry if I made you unhappy.'

She originally came to me with a problem in her joints which medically was incurable. Gradually, the Lord has been healing her joints as she has learnt to draw closer to Him. There was a step forward that day when, under the power of the Holy Spirit, she was able to forgive her father from the depth of her heart.

Fairly often a woman comes here who has been desperately rejected in childhood and who finds it impossible to forgive her parents. She may feel conscious of the resentment and the anger within her. Or she may not even be aware of them. But these feelings will be working like a spiritual cancer within her, and she will need to let them go. One has to be constantly on the lookout for such situations. For if we are unable to forgive those who have hurt us, it means we are not in a position to receive the forgiveness and the healing which the Lord longs to give us. 'Forgive us our trespasses as we forgive them . . .'

Sometimes I ask people to imagine how they would

feel if they were to see someone they loved suffering deeply, and if they were unable themselves to relieve that suffering. I ask them, 'Would you not then say that your heart was bleeding for that person?' People understand the meaning of that expression. One can try to help them to see that, while they were suffering as a small child (or whenever), Jesus loved them so much that His own heart was bleeding for them.

One can then go further. 'If you have this hardness and unforgiveness in your heart now, it is depriving you of the peace of God. Indeed it is denying you the joy which the Lord loves to share with His children. His heart is still bleeding for you, now, as you continue to suffer from those past hurts. Do you realise that Jesus loves you deeply, that He is loving you deeply right now at this very moment? And can you not see that He is therefore suffering with you in your own pain?'

We may then say, 'Shut your eyes and look up into the light of Jesus. Picture His light shining down on you. Open your heart to Him, and let the light of His love pour into your heart. Let go and allow yourself to love Him. Let go and share the hurts of the past with Jesus. Thank Him in your heart that He is at this very minute suffering with you in your pain, and that therefore He is sharing your suffering with you. Let go of the pain, and let it go to Jesus. Can't you see He is standing there holding His hands out in front of you, and longing to take the pain from you? Can't you let it go to Him? Can't you trust Him, and accept His love for you?'

We may then ask the person, 'Does Jesus love your mother and your father with the same perfect love He has for you? Were they happy? You don't know how much they suffered in their early lives before you were born, and what suffering caused them to be so unkind to you. Doesn't Jesus' heart bleed for them in their suffering in just the same way that His heart has been bleeding for you in yours? Can't you see that Jesus is longing to share their suffering, and, if they would only let Him, to relieve them of their pain and take it to Himself? Can't you see that Jesus is longing for them to turn to Him, and to repent of their unkindness to you, so that He can give them His forgiveness, and they can feel the burden of their unkindness lifted off them?'

Perhaps by now the person is ready for the question: 'If Jesus loves your parents so much, is He not longing to relieve them of the pain they must have suffered, in their own early lives? If He is longing to forgive them, can you, yourself, now follow Jesus and forgive your parents yourself?'

Only yesterday I was ministering to a woman in her forties who had this very problem. As I led up to this last question, and eventually asked her whether she could forgive her parents, there was no hesitation. She just said very quietly, 'Yes, I do forgive them now.' We prayed down the power of the Holy Spirit of Jesus on her. We prayed for her healing from her emotional hurts, and when we had finished she said, with a lovely smile, 'I feel that a tremendous load has just been lifted off me.'

My wife, Audrey had a horrid experience as a child when her tonsils were removed. The surgeon and the anaesthetist had come out to operate on her at home. No-one she knew was present when she was put down on the makeshift operating table. She cried out for help and her nanny appeared for a moment at the door. But the nurse pushed her out and shut the door in her face. Audrey was alone with these strange people. She remembers screaming with fear, which turned to panic as the rubber mask was jammed down over her face until she lost consciousness.

Audrey is a very balanced person, but she still dreaded the moments when she re-experienced that terror. She asked one of the team here to pray for her. As they did, the picture of herself lying on that makeshift operating table with the rubber mask being shoved over her face, gently and slowly receded further and further away into the distance. Never since has she been worried by recollections of that traumatic day in her childhood.

Perhaps that occasion was somewhat unusual, in that the fading away of the memory was quietly accomplished by the action of the Holy Spirit without introducing the presence and the comfort of Jesus. Usually it is the experience of His love and of being safe in His hands which washes away the hurt. Psychologists tell us that something experienced in the imagination can have the same effect on the mind as the experience of something which actually happened. This seems to be as near as one can get to a scientific evaluation of the effect of healing of memories.

There is no way, of course, in which we can quantify emotional healing. The process is subjective in the mind of the person being prayed for. But it is real.

The person who is praying cannot just switch on such healing. All we can do is commit the situation to the Lord and ask Him, through His Holy Spirit, to lead in perfect love.

When Jesus preached in the synagogue at Nazaret, He read from Isaiah and applied to Himself the prophecy that He had come to proclaim freedom for the prisoners, and to release the oppressed (Lk 4.18).

One of the saddest sessions I have had was with a

homosexual – and one of the most fulfilling was with another homosexual. The first was a boy of nineteen. His partner, some twelve years older, had already been to see me once, and I had felt that we were making some progress. Now it was the younger man's turn. I remember asking him if he wanted to be set free from his homosexuality. 'I long to be free,' he said, 'I long to be like other men. I long to be able to marry and have children and a home of my own.'

I asked him then what he expected to happen when we started to pray. There was a look of infinite sadness in his eyes as he looked up and said, 'What am I expecting to happen? Why, nothing.'

We prayed, and of course nothing did happen. And he persuaded his partner not to come again.

But there was another occasion when a homosexual man came to see me. I explained to him that homosexuality was both a sin which needed to be forgiven (Rom 1.27) and a sickness which needed to be healed. He confessed it as a sin and asked the Lord to forgive him, and we then discussed how the Lord heals. Some people assert that with the homosexual there is hormonal imbalance. I told him that we had seen the Lord heal most things here and, if he had a hormonal imbalance, there was no reason why the Lord should not heal this. We prayed for him.

We talked about the only two alternatives for the Christian where sex is concerned, either the joy of celibacy, or a perfect Christian marriage. He said he had no feeling that celibacy was for him.

As he left, I encouraged him to seek the company of girls, just to get used to being with them, and to regard a girl simply as another companion.

Some two years later, he came to see me again. He

started by telling me that, as he had left the mission, he had felt that I didn't know what I was talking about. 'The last thing I wanted,' he said, 'was to have anything to do with any girl.'

'But the reason I've come here to see you again today is not to ask for prayer about my homosexuality. That has been healed. My reason for coming today is that I want you to pray for my fiancée and me in our forthcoming marriage.'

There was another lovely occasion involving a homosexual. He had cut himself off from his family and his friends to go and live with his male partner 'somewhere in Brighton'. A Christian girl he knew had felt that the Lord was telling her to find him. Imagine her faith that she should take a train to Brighton with the objective of finding this man 'somewhere.'

But the Lord was in it. Within an hour and a half she bumped into him in the street. He was taken aback, not only to see her but also to hear how she had come to find him. She brought him here for ministry. I have not seen him since, but I feel certain that in the period of ministry and prayer here, the Lord set him free.

There are few boys who are not attracted to other boys at some stage in their teens. Mercifully when I was at school we were taught quite clearly that to indulge such an attraction was wrong, and my friends and I never did. But how easy it must be today for boys who are taught that homosexuality is an acceptable alternative to fall into the trap and start indulging in it.

Much propaganda is put out nowadays by homosexual and lesbian groups. I don't believe, however, that it is ever possible for a man or woman to find true satisfaction other than in a permanent relationship with someone of the other sex.

Moreover, the idea of two people of the same sex committing themselves permanently to each other is usually a myth. I have seen it written by a professional psychotherapist who works widely with homosexuals that usually after two or three months together their eyes are turning to others of their own sex, and for them to stay together for two years is statistically unusual (Gerard van den Aardweg, *Homosexuality and Hope*).

A Christian woman wrote to me recently, quoting her son of fifteen who is certainly not a believer. 'Many of my friends,' he had said to his mother, 'deliberately pervert themselves just to be different.'

10

Supping with the devil?

Every now and then, someone comes to the mission declaring, 'I need deliverance.' Usually they are wrong.

Many people who think they have an unclean spirit in them are simply suffering the kind of 'oppression' which most Christians meet with at some time. If you are constantly battling with some particular temptation and are finding it very difficult to get free, it is easy to think that there must be some unclean spirit within you. Once you entertain the idea, Satan will try to convince you, not only that this is in fact the case, but that, of yourself, you can't get free. You may then go to those you believe have a deliverance ministry. Each of them in turn fails to set you free, for the simple reason that there is in fact no unclean spirit there to cast out.

How, then, does one help such a person? We always take the sword of the Holy Spirit (Eph 6.17) and, in the name of Jesus, cut them free from whatever has been oppressing them. But often the Lord requires something more. He wants us to reach out and make the effort ourselves, learning, as we go, to draw on the power of His Holy Spirit within us. It will be necessary to pray against the particular temptation which is so besetting the person, and then to help them to pray for the opposite virtue. For example, if it is a sexual sin, the person will need to pray for purity and that with the Lord's help, he or she may keep their body holy before the Lord. Set the seal on that prayer by thanking the Lord in faith that He has heard it and that He will now be answering it.

Unfortunately some Christians assume that if they are stuck, in ministering to someone, it must be because the person has a demon. If they proceed on these lines they may damage the person they are trying to help.

We had an instance of this with our own daughter Caroline. In her early thirties she suffered from rheumatism and went to a Christian man I knew who had been in the healing ministry for many years. In prayer with Caroline he took the authority of Jesus and instructed a spirit of rheumatism to leave her. There was no apparent manifestation of anything going, but he assured Caroline that it would have gone.

But the rheumatism didn't go. Having been told that the problem lay with a spirit of rheumatism, Caroline rang up from her home in considerable distress, saying: 'Daddy, does this mean that I've still got this horrid thing wandering around inside me?' If Caroline had been a less well balanced person, and if she had had no-one to turn to, one can imagine how the fear of having an unclean spirit 'wandering around inside her' could have come to prey on her mind. I had to tell her quite firmly that I knew she was not demonised, whatever my friend had prayed for. One may rebuke the sickness in a person, as Jesus did with the fever in

Peter's mother-in-law (Lk 4.39). That is, however, different from casting out an unclean spirit.

Recently we had another case which could have been tragic. A girl in her late twenties came to me for prayer saying that everything in her life seemed to be going wrong. As we talked through what had been happening, one could see only too easily why she had come to this conclusion.

I prayed robustly with her. A couple of weeks later I had a lovely letter from her, saying that although it was a continuing battle to live in the victory of Jesus, she was managing to do this, and now everything seemed gradually to be going right in her life. How I rejoiced for her sake when I read that letter.

Then she came here one morning without an appointment and very distressed. She said she had 'been for deliverance' two days before, and that 'they' had cast something out, but that it had returned and, in desperation, she had then attempted to take her life.

I knew, from having prayed with her, that there was no unclean spirit in her. The people who had tried 'a deliverance ministry' on her had been mistaken in their approach and had very nearly been responsible for a ghastly tragedy. Clearly she had been emotionally upset when she went to them for help, and it was easy to see how, as they prayed with her, her emotional problems of the moment had been eased.

But nothing lasting had been achieved. Small wonder that a few hours later the emotional problems re-emerged. Now, however, the girl was in a worse state than before, because she had now been told that she was demonised.

Normally we don't see people without an appointment, except at one of our healing services. But mercifully Audrey was able to see her at once. She left calm and at peace.

Some Christians tend to see 'demons' whenever they are having difficulty knowing how to minister to someone who is emotionally upset. Yet unclean spirits do exist. We never refer to them as 'demons', for that has become an emotive word. We may use the words in the original Greek text, 'unclean spirits', or we may just refer to them as 'squalid little nuisances', which is all they are.

In the same way, we never refer to someone as 'being possessed', an emotive expression. If someone believes they are 'possessed', they may claim that they are no longer responsible for their own lives. I don't believe that this is ever the case. At some stage after we die, each of us is going to stand before the Lord to give an account of our life in this world (Heb 9.27). I don't believe the excuse will be accepted if we say, 'Look, Jesus, I'm so sorry that I didn't make much of my life on earth, but You do understand, don't You, that I was possessed by an unclean spirit, so I couldn't have done any more, could I?'

I believe that if someone is 'demonised' – the word used frequently in the New Testament – they may suffer stronger temptation, perhaps much stronger, in the area covered by that particular unclean spirit. But the decision whether to give in to that temptation is still their own responsibility.

Every now and then, someone comes to us who has been deep into witchcraft and satanism, perhaps for many years. However, they still have the choice to come out of it and to be set free, if they so desire. It will be a hard struggle. Some will find the struggle too hard and will sink back into the evil morass from which they sought to escape. But they are free to take the decision either way themselves, and the responsibility remains theirs.

In our ministry we never go looking for unclean spirits. We always assume that a person is not demonised until we have evidence that they are. We want to concentrate all the time on helping the person to get his or her eyes onto Jesus.

We have had many instances of people being set free from unclean spirits. Often the first we have known about the person being demonised was when there was a manifestation of the unclean spirit or spirits leaving. We can take deliverance in our stride as we continue to minister to the person.

In many ways, getting an unclean spirit out of someone is rather like getting rid of leeches. Anyone who has lived in the tropics will know that if you walk through long wet grass with bare legs, you will probably pick up a few leeches. They are about an inch long, have very sharp teeth and bury their heads in your legs. Then they gradually suck your blood until their body, which had seemed as thin as a piece of cotton, gradually swells into a little balloon. Then they drop off and spend a period of time digesting your blood until they are once more ready to attach themselves to a person or an animal and begin the process again.

They don't hurt, but I would rather keep my blood to myself than share it with a few leeches. Moreover, it is no good trying to pull them off, because their bodies just come apart from their heads. Their heads remain in your leg and go septic. I found that the easiest way of getting rid of leeches was to puff on a cigarette until it glowed red and then to apply the cigarette end to the tail of the leech.

In a way, it is like that with unclean spirits. If you think a person may be demonised, you can run through half a dozen tests. If there is no reaction, you will be fairly safe in telling the person that they are not demonised. This can be a real relief to them. Moreover you can run through the tests without even telling them what you are doing.

Often we simply use our discernment and say firmly to the person, 'You just aren't demonised; stop worrying.' People worry far too much about demons.

If, however, as you apply one of the tests, you find there is some bizarre manifestation, then it may be right to press on, applying the same test, until you make it too hot for the unclean spirits to stay there. Then it leaves the person – in much the same manner as the leech drops off when you make it too hot for it by holding a lighted cigarette to the end of its body.

Yet even if there is some bizarre manifestation it doesn't necessarily mean that the person has an unclean spirit. If a person has been deeply hurt emotionally, they may groan, or cry out, or, indeed, behave strangely as the hurt surfaces under the power of the Holy Spirit. There may be an unclean spirit there, or there may not.

It is important in ministry to have the humility to realise that one may have got it wrong, and not to press on obstinately, convinced that one must be right. Much harm can be done that way.

Unclean spirits may react to mention of the Blood of Jesus. They have enough intelligence to know quite well that the power of their master, Satan, was broken when Jesus shed His blood on the cross; sometimes they so dread the mention of the Blood of Jesus that they will flee. Sometimes what gets them is someone praying in tongues. There is real spiritual power in that language, and again they dread it. On other occasions it may be the mention of the name of Jesus, for they know well the power that there is in His name. Again, it may be holy oil which 'tickles them up', or sprinkling with holy water. It may be the sign of the cross made on the person, or it may be the chalice at the communion service. A person who is heavily demonised usually cannot take the cup, for, once the wine is consecrated, in spiritual terms it becomes the blood of Jesus. We have seen someone who was quite heavily demonised seize the communion cup in a sudden outburst of rage and hurl it across the room. Finally, as one prays down the light and the power of the Holy Spirit, one may make it too hot for them so that they go.

Timing is important. Usually, if deliverance is involved, there is healing to be done too, perhaps spiritually as well as emotionally. We need to discern the sequence in which, in His wisdom, the Holy Spirit wants to minister. If however there is an unclean spirit, and if in the Lord's timing it is the right moment to set the person free, the unclean spirit will usually react to one or other of these tests. You then press on with whatever has provoked the unclean spirit to manifest itself, whether it be using the Name of Jesus, referring to His Blood, the sign of the cross, until eventually the unclean spirit goes. Sometimes they are really noisy when they leave and the person gives a wild shriek. But often it is something much quieter, like a fit of coughing, or a yawn or exhalation which indicates that the thing has gone.

Occasionally, we find it necessary to get the unclean spirit to disclose its name, as Jesus did with 'Legion' (Mk 5.9). But usually, when they are ready to go, all one need do is command them to get out in the Name of Jesus. We always then instruct them in His Name to go to Him to be dealt with by Him. We know a girl who, with her flatmate, was ministering deliverance to someone who had come to them. They got the thing out but they forgot to tell it to go to Jesus, and it then just hopped into one of the girls themselves and it was five days before they got it out of her. That time, they made no mistake and instructed it in the Name of Jesus to go straight to Him.

We never shout, whether in deliverance or in any other area of ministry. People often comment on how quiet and peaceful the ministry is here. All you need to do is to speak the word of God (not necessarily verbatim from the scriptures). You then rest on Isaiah's assurance when he heard God saying, 'My word will not return to me empty but will accomplish what I desire' (Is 55.11).

We have a rule that where deliverance is concerned, we have two of us there, who have had experience of this type of ministry. Before we start we cover everyone, in prayer, with the blood of Jesus. But there are times when one is into a deliverance situation before one knows what is happening. I remember praying with a young man – I forget whether it was praying in tongues or reference to the blood of Jesus which I used – when he instantly fell to the ground, writhed like a snake and kept spewing out phlegm. (They seldom vomit, though phlegm is quite common.) I made it as hot as I could for the unclean things, until they all left him.

The first time Audrey and I got involved in deliverance, it was certainly not for our own choosing. I was still working in the City. Someone rang at ten in the evening, saying that a mutual friend was in a trance and would we go round and help. Audrey said quite firmly that I had to catch the 8.02 train to London the next morning and we couldn't come. Why didn't they contact their friend's minister? The answer was that they had tried him and he was away. Then came the challenging words, 'But we thought Andy was an ordained minister.'

We talked it over for five minutes. We felt the Lord was saying, 'Are you going to be obedient to me or not?' We realised then that we had to go. The house was about five miles away. As we hadn't the least idea what to do, we both prayed the whole way in tongues.

We found the woman sitting on the floor, with her eyes open and quite clearly in a trance. The friend was there, and also the woman's husband, who was an unbeliever and an alcoholic. I sat beside the woman on the floor, telling her about Jesus, telling her about His love, and telling her about his death on the cross. Nothing seemed to register. I then happened to mention that, in dying on the cross, He had shed His blood for her. She jumped as if I had touched her with a live electric wire.

I think it took about half an hour. By then several unclean spirits had clearly gone and she was out of the trance and behaving quite normally. We asked the Lord to fill with His Holy Spirit the spaces which had been left when the unclean spirits left and we then sat with them all, over a cup of coffee for a further half an hour to make sure that she was completely relaxed and normal again. Then we left. I can't remember how long it all took but I caught the 8.02 train the following morning.

We saw her twice more before she became completely free and each time a number of unclean spirits had to be cast out. She showed us her Bible with curious marks on the back. It was as if human fingerprints had been burnt into the leather cover. She told us that this was, in fact, what had happened. Sometimes, when someone who is demonised comes into contact with something which is holy, there is a release of heat, and her fingers had burnt the finger marks into the cover of her Bible. She told us how, one morning, she had dreamt that the crucifix in her hall had been broken. She had come down to breakfast, and found the crucifix lying on the floor in pieces. Her real fear had been that she would kill, not only herself, but also her husband and her children, such was the strength she had recognised in the unclean spirits she knew were lurking within her.

As we ministered to her, she would crouch in terror on the floor in a corner of the room and howl like a dog. After three sessions, she was completely free. But the end of the story really came two weeks after that. After seeing what the Lord had done for his wife, her husband gave his life to Jesus and gave up the drinking which had plagued him for years. Then we saw them both at a Christian meeting and, although they were in their forties and with grown-up children, they were so clearly enjoying being together that they might have been a newly-engaged couple. I caught Audrey's eye, and as we saw them, we both murmured a heartfelt prayer of thanks to Jesus.

Then there was Aileen (not her real name), who had been rejected by her parents and had gone to live with her grandparents, where she had had a happy childhood until the age of twelve. Then her grandmother died and her grandfather committed her to a local woman. What he did not know was that the woman was involved in witchcraft.

She explained to us something of what was involved in satanic ceremonies: 'These six people in this part of the temple give protection to those who are outside the circle. They in turn are protected by the six over there in their two groups.'

'What do they need protection from?' I asked. Aileen shook her head. 'I can't remember,' she answered.

'The very person they are seeking protection from,' I suggested, 'is the person they are themselves worshipping, namely Satan himself!' As the saying goes, you need a very long spoon indeed if you are going to sup with the devil.'

Some while after she was taken in by them, Aileen and her boy partner found themselves the central figures in the black mass, the culminating point in the worship of Satan. She was ushered into the 'temple' where all the satanist devotees were gathered, wearing a long black shroud and nothing else underneath.

Many years later, she told us that she had to break free from that satanist community because she was sickened by all the senseless cruelty and destruction. A number of girls were brought into Aileen's community each year. Most of them, she said, finished up as prostitutes. She knew of five who had tried to get free. Each of them had finally committed suicide. Once one gives oneself deliberately, and over a period of time, to the worship of Satan, it is very, very hard to get free. Aileen was the sixth.

For eight years, Aileen was forced to live in that community. Every night they were hypnotised. She had little formal education, but she was trained in satanism, voodoo, black magic and spiritualism. She was a practising medium for ten years. 'Voodoo', she told us, 'is the most powerful of them all.' When she eventually came to us, she had been involved in the community, off and on, for some thirty years.

A Christian friend used to bring her to see us at the mission. She said it always took a lot of coaxing to get Aileen here, she was so nervous of coming. Every time when we met her at the front door, she would try and turn back, but we usually succeeded in coaxing her into my room, where Audrey and I ministered together, but she was clearly terrified. They offered her money running into thousands of pounds a year to stay with them, and on one occasion a kidnap attempt was only narrowly averted.

People who are demonised react in different ways. With her we used the gift of tongues a lot, and also the sign of the cross. We also used holy water. As we often do here, we just drew some cold water from the tap in the kitchen, and then we blessed it. Once when we sprinkled her, even though she was wearing a leather coat, she cried out, 'You're scalding me!' Such is often the reaction when a person who is demonised comes into contact with something which has been blessed.

Often the unclean spirits themselves would cry out, 'Come on now, Aileen, it's time to go home.' Sometimes they even added, 'They've done enough damage for one afternoon!' Audrey and I were fighting a war on two fronts. We were seeking, through the power of the Holy Spirit, to strengthen the resolve in Aileen to throw off the legacy of evil. At the same time, and again in the power of the Holy Spirit, we were coming against the evil itself.

The main reason for the ministry taking so long was that Aileen had been programmed through those years of hypnotism so that she was literally unable to hear or even read the name of Jesus. When we said the name of Jesus, she heard it as 'Satan' or 'Lucifer'. Indeed on one occasion, she seriously began to mistrust us. 'But I thought you were on the other side', she said, 'Why do you keep talking to me about Satan?' We replied that we were not talking about Satan, but that we were referring to Jesus. 'There you are! You said his name again!' she retorted.

As anyone who has been involved in this kind of ministry well knows, the power is in the name of Jesus. We realised that if we were debarred from mentioning His name, we were put in a position where, in a sense, we were ministering to Aileen with our hands tied. Well do I remember the occasion when, after a full night of ministry, she suddenly looked up and said, 'Who on earth is Jesus?' (The question was in fact put in more forceful words than that!) But we were thrilled. It was the first time she had been able to hear the name of Jesus.

But even after that, she had difficulty in reading the Bible. Each time she came to the name of Jesus she read it as 'Satan'. One could see the effect of that endless hypnotism all too clearly. In the sitting room upstairs here we have a copy of Salvador Dali's picture of Jesus' crucifixion. She asked Audrey why we had a picture-frame on the wall with no picture in it. After she came free, she stared and stared at the picture. 'So that's what it really is,' she said, adding: 'That man suffered even more than I did.'

That occasion, when she was able to hear the name of Jesus for the first time, was the first real breakthrough. The second was when eventually, and after what seemed endless cajoling, she was able to summon up the spiritual strength to ask Jesus to cleanse her. I don't think I will ever forget the halting words she mumbled, 'Jesus, cleanse me!'

Very early in her initiation into that satanic community, she was 'married' to a boy of her own age. There was no physical consummation of that marriage. Indeed the leaders deliberately perverted the boy to make him homosexual. They were 'married' before the black altar by the cutting of a finger on each of their left hands, and then the binding together of their hands so that their blood intermingled. Later he rose, as Aileen told us, to be one of the satanic leaders. On the occasion of the second breakthrough, when Aileen was at last able to pray out loud, 'Jesus, cleanse me', she told us that she felt a sudden severe pain in her heart. She looked up and said, 'He's had a heart attack.' The following morning she rang and told us that he had in fact had a heart attack at that time.

When Aileen finally came through and became completely free at about 4.30 a.m. she turned to us and said, 'He's died.' Subsequently, she learnt that he had died at that time.

It took some sixty hours of ministry before, in the power of Jesus, we finally won through. She explained that the powers of darkness are at their most active in the middle of the night. The last three sessions began after lunch, and went right through until daybreak the next day. It was summer so the dawn came fairly early. But this was exceptional. Normally it is a mistake to go on ministering when you are tired.

About 2.30 a.m. during the final session Aileen asked if she could go to our chapel in the basement. I wasn't sure what was going to happen, and as I opened the chapel door, I stood behind her. As she slowly took one step into the chapel she was blown backwards off her feet. I caught her as she fell. As she lay on the floor her feet were some five feet behind where the 'explosion' had occurred. There had been no sound. This is an example of what may happen when evil comes into contact with the light of Christ.

We returned upstairs and eventually Aileen was able to tell us the names of six voodoo spirits which she had voluntarily invited to enter her during a satanist ceremony when she was in her teens. She had not been told the names of the spirits but somehow, under the power of the Holy Spirit, she was able to give us their names. Moreover she was able to give us the right sequence in which they had to be cast out, for otherwise, she said, they would have linked up again. They knew when they were beaten. They knew by then that they were up against the power of the risen Christ. They could not stand the sign of the cross by which their master's power had been broken, or reference to the blood of Jesus by which his power had been destroyed. We sent them to Jesus to be dealt with by Him.

Audrey was then given a word of knowledge that Aileen needed to repent. She asked Jesus to forgive her her sins. Clearly her repentance was from the heart, and we know that when we confess our sins genuinely, Jesus is faithful and just to forgive us our sins and to cleanse us from all unrighteousness (1 Jn 1.9 AV). Yet something clearly remained to be done.

Again, Audrey was given the necessary discernment. 'I believe, Aileen,' she said, 'that you need to command any remaining unclean spirits to go, yourself, in the name of Jesus.' Aileen took His authority and robustly commanded any such spirits to leave. I think it was I who then realised that the sixty hours of ministry were at an end. 'Aileen, I believe you're free,' I said. At last all those hours of ministry, spreading over several months, were finished.

'Ought we to have the bread and the wine?' Aileen asked, so we had a little informal communion service together. Had there been any more problems she would have been unable to take the sacraments.

'Can we go down to the chapel?' Aileen asked. The three of us knelt before the altar, pouring out our hearts to Jesus in gratitude and praise. And this was only a couple of hours after the 'explosion'. The three of us wept.

A day or two later, she rang us in distress. 'They' had made a wax doll in her image, and were sticking pins into it. She had sharp shooting pains in her chest. We saw her that same day. We took the sword of the Holy Spirit, which is the Word of God (Eph 6.17) and as we spoke forth the word of God released her from the evil power they had tried to put upon her. As we finished praying I said, 'I think you may find the evil power will boomerang onto the man who tried to put it on you.' The following morning, they rang up angrily accusing her, and saying, 'What the *hell* have you been doing to −?'

Aileen's story was exceptional. It seems right, however, to include it as an example of what can be involved when a person gives himself to Satan and is subsequently ministered to.

Mankind has always been tempted to try to sup with the devil. Aileen was fascinated by the power she saw. People may be drawn in by promises of power, money, or sexual conquests. They can be intrigued by the mystery, the excitement, the challenge of playing one person against another, fascinated by the influence and

the control they can have over other people. But once
caught up in the web, it is very, very hard to break free.
The power of evil is real. If it was not, satanism might
be silly, but there would be little harm in it.

Recently we have had to minister to two young men,
each of them now fine Christians. Each of them, however, had been involved in hard rock music several
years ago. Each had listened endlessly to tapes of such
music with satanic backtracking – if you played the
tape backwards, you heard words like, 'Satan I love
you, I give myself to you.' It is well known that the
unconscious mind picks up such subliminal messages.
They told us of the mass hypnotism which takes place
at hard rock concerts, the place packed with young
devotees all 'headbanging'; that is, jerking their heads
violently up and down in time with the music. Both
these young men were demonised when they came to
us, and had to be set free in the power of Jesus.

We draw two conclusions. We read in the Bible of the
'unforgiveable sin' (1 Jn 5.16). I find it hard to conceive
of any sin which Aileen had not committed during those
thirty years. Yet we both saw clearly that she had
received the cleansing and the forgiveness of Jesus.
Aileen now is a stronger Christian than most of us will
ever be. She has been set free from the evil, and she has
been set free from the fear which always accompanies a
commitment to Satan. No longer is she now, in her own
words, 'petrified of death'. She looks forward to the
time when Jesus will take her to be with Him forever.

The other conclusion we draw is this. Don't get
involved in this kind of deliverance ministry unless the
Lord quite definitely leads you into it. It can be dangerous. A woman came to us once who had been ministered to previously, and unsuccessfully, for deliverance

by her minister. He should have known better. After one such time of ministry she had been found by her friend walking down the middle of the road at midnight in a trance. Only by the mercy of God was she saved from what could easily have been a fatal accident.

We have the instance in Acts when the seven sons of Sceva tried to cast out an unclean spirit. In this case the spirit actually turned on them and the attempted deliverance ministry finished with the seven of them fleeing for their lives (Ac 19.14).

If, however, one gets involved in this ministry under the direct guiding of the Holy Spirit, and under the protection of Jesus, then there is nothing to fear. Audrey and I used to remark to each other, every time Aileen had gone, on the complete absence of fear in us.

But if one ventures to meddle in such matters other than under the protection of Jesus and the power of His blood, and guided by His Holy Spirit, it is like playing around with the wiring of a house without turning off the electric current. It can be very dangerous, both for oneself and for the person one is trying to minister to. There are all too many cases nowadays of people having been damaged by the attentions of 'amateur exorcists'.

11

The Language of the Holy Spirit

As we saw earlier on, when Paul listed the gifts of the Holy Spirit (1 Cor 12.9) he included gifts of healing in the plural. At the mission we share with others what the Lord seems to have shown us here, and which we see working. We would never want to convey, however, that if you do it differently then you are doing it wrong. You may have another of the Lord's gifts of healing and that may give Him the same glory as ours does – and be just as effective.

Having reiterated that, I want to share some thoughts on the gift of tongues. Jesus is recorded as having said, 'These signs will follow those that believe . . .', (Mk 16.17, AV). He didn't say that these signs might follow those that believed, nor did He say that these signs would follow some of those who believed. He said, 'These signs will follow those that believe'.

At first sight this would not seem to be borne out by 1 Corinthians 12–14. But if we read those three chapters together, we see that Paul is addressing himself there to the church, which is the body of Christ. Obviously, it would be chaotic if everyone spoke together in tongues at a fellowship meeting!

We are concerned now, however, with the gift of tongues as used in one's own private prayer time and we remember how Paul wrote 'I would like every one of you to speak in tongues' (1 Cor 14.5). He goes on to see this practice as edifying, as we pray quietly in our own quiet times.

I believe the Lord in His love wants to give us this gift. It is a help in worshipping Him, it is a help in combatting Satan, and it is a language of real spiritual power. Jesus said 'If you, then, though you are evil, know how to give good gifts to your children, how much more will your Father in heaven give the Holy Spirit to those who ask Him!' (Lk 11.13). I find it difficult to understand how a God of love would want to hold back something which is good from those He loved.

But timing comes into the question. I received the gift of tongues when I was forty-nine. I might therefore have been forgiven if at any time during what was nearly my first half century I had declared, 'He does not want to give me that gift.' If I had said that, I would have been wrong. If I had been going to express an opinion on the subject, the correct thing to have said would have been, 'The Lord has not given it to me yet, because in His view I am not yet ready to receive it.'

In fact, most people we pray for receive that gift at once. The other day, I was praying with twelve people together for that gift. Eleven received it. The twelfth did not – but then she never opened her mouth. How can one speak any language with closed lips!

But there are those who don't receive. Perhaps what holds them back is the fear of venturing out, to speak in a language they haven't learnt. Perhaps it is a lack of faith, or perhaps it is that the Lord in His love is just saying quietly, 'I long to give you this gift but I'm afraid you're not quite ready for it yet.'

Audrey and I were doing a teaching and healing weekend near Midhurst. A woman came to me saying she would love to have the gift of tongues. 'But', she added, 'I've been seeking it for eleven years now. Many people have prayed for me, and I haven't received it.'

I told her not to worry, and I told her some of the more obvious points about the gift of tongues, all of which I am sure she had heard many times before. We then prayed, and she didn't receive anything.

'I should forget it,' I said. It was one of those lovely frosty days with the sun shining in a pale blue sky. 'Go out into the garden,' I said, 'and enjoy this winter afternoon, and forget all about tongues.'

When I saw her at supper she was smiling broadly. She rushed up excitedly to tell me what had happened. 'I did as you told me,' she said. 'I had a lovely walk round the garden – and I returned to the house praising the Lord in the language of the Holy Spirit!'

A common difficulty is that people may think they are just making up the sounds which they are producing. They may have been brought up to regard speaking in tongues as desperately spiritual. The strange words they are producing seem on the face of it to be anything but spiritual. Yet I believe that, if one perseveres, the Lord will 'grow' what might have started as fabricated words into the gift of tongues if those words are used to praise Him and worship Him.

One woman who received the gift of tongues still refused, a year later, to accept that it was that gift. Yet she found making those sounds positively helpful.

I once prayed for a man, who had been a pre-war

tennis star at Wimbledon, to receive the gift of tongues. We prayed together that the Lord would give him this gift. I instructed his tongue in the Name of Jesus to be set free. Then, while I gave him a lead, praying in my language of the Holy Spirit, I told him to make whatever sounds came to his mind.

'Oo, ah, um! Oo, ah, um!' were the sounds which came forth. Quite obviously, he was not praying in tongues, but I encouraged him to keep going. 'Keep on!' I said. It was fascinating, about half a minute later, to hear the words change. It was rather like listening to the different note of a car engine as one changes gear. As the change came, he began praying fluently in a language he had never learned.

I believe that Satan counterfeits all the gifts of the Holy Spirit. We were praying with a girl who was demonised and we encouraged her to pray in tongues. It was a harsh sound which came from her lips. Moreover, she was in bondage to it. She wasn't free to stop and start at her own will. We told her in the name of Jesus to stop it, and she stopped.

We then released her in the name of Jesus from that hold which the false tongue had on her, and we asked the Lord to give her the real language of His Holy Spirit. In a few moments she was quietly praying in a lovely melodious new language of her own, completely in control in that she was able to start and stop at her own will.

Prayer in the language of the Holy Spirit is, however, a prayer which has spiritual power. David Wilkerson in New York and Jackie Pullinger in Hong Kong have ministries to heroin addicts. They have found that as they lead the heroin addicts to Jesus, and as they pray with them to receive the baptism of the

Holy Spirit and the gift of tongues, they can come off heroin, without medication, and without suffering the appalling pain which normally follows, if prayer continues to be offered in the language of the Holy Spirit.

Yet I remember the evening Audrey and I were having supper with a Christian friend at home. She had asked a woman friend of hers who was also involved in the healing ministry to come and meet us. As we were talking, I discerned, rightly, that she did not have the gift of tongues. I thought I would be helping her if I expanded a little on the wonderful help which that language is, and the power which it releases. Looking back, I think I was probably being a little patronising.

After supper, we got onto the subject of praying for people with multiple sclerosis. 'Do you find that people with MS respond to prayer when you pray for them?' the other woman asked. I explained that actually we hadn't seen any response when praying with people with MS. At that stage, we hadn't.

'Oh, that's sad,' she replied, 'We see real improvement when we pray for MS sufferers.' While each of us can be thankful for the way the Lord chooses to work through our individual ministries, we need to remember constantly that He is sovereign, and that, if He chooses to work in a different way through other people, then to Him be all the glory.

12

Why Aren't they Healed?

I know of no-one in the healing ministry who would ever claim a hundred per cent success rate when praying with people for their healing. Consequently, one must in honesty look at the question, 'What has gone wrong when they aren't healed?'

Many people were deeply worried when David Watson died. Thousands of Christians were praying for him to be healed. Yet he died at a relatively young age. But all of us need to die sometime, and I felt the Lord gave His own answer to David before his death with those words, 'I want you to realise, David, that my relationship of love with you is the most important thing of all.'

In many ways, the death of a Christian is the most complete and perfect form of healing. It is lovely to think of David, released from the asthma which had always plagued him, no longer afflicted with cancer, and now in perfect harmony and joy with the Jesus he loved so dearly.

Others will have read in *Joni* how an American girl broke her neck in a diving accident at the age of seventeen and has been in a wheelchair ever since. Again, she had many, many people praying for her recovery and, speaking physically, the Lord has not healed her. Yet the Lord in His mercy used those many prayers to do a tremendous work in her spiritually.

Through enabling her to come to terms with her disability, He was able to release her into a very powerful ministry, helping tens of thousands of people who are similarly confined to wheelchairs. Indeed many others have benefited from her wonderfully strong and positive approach to life. She is now genuinely able to thank the Lord that He didn't heal her physically because He had something even better for her. One evening Joni was on the stage of the Royal Albert Hall, only a few yards away from us. She looked radiant as she sat there in her wheelchair. I simply couldn't feel sorry for her!

Then we have known people who have been healed physically as soon as they have been released from a binding sin, and before we had even prayed for the physical healing. There must be instances where a person has been bound similarly by sin, but the one praying for them has failed to perceive this and has asked instead for the physical healing – only to find that nothing has happened. Quite often one of us may see no result because, quite simply, we have not perceived the right thing to pray for. The Lord may have been longing to heal, but in His divine plan there was something else He knew needed to be put right first.

The mystery deepens. Many people in the healing ministry will say that sometimes the Lord wants to heal a person through another specific person, and He won't heal them through the prayers of someone else. In one of his books Francis MacNutt tells of an ex-prize fighter who became a Christian. He learnt that God still heals today. Being a man of action, he rushed round to the local hospital, hurried into the nearest ward, and proceeded to lay hands on one patient after another.

He was told to leave, and wandered back disconsolately to his home. 'Why did You let me down?' he demanded of God. It took him some while to calm down sufficiently for him to be able to hear what the Lord was saying in reply. 'Who actually told you to go and heal those specific people?' the small inner voice seemed to be saying to him.

We have seen that there are times when the perfect plan of God is to release His healing power on someone, but after a delay. While they are waiting for their healing, He will be stretching their faith so that He can take the opportunity to grow them into greater spiritual maturity as well as healing them physically. There must be times, however, when the person is not sufficiently resolute to hold on in faith to the healing which they have asked for. How sad the Lord must be then, for in that case neither of those objectives will have been achieved, and the person will remain unchanged, both physically and spiritually.

There are also times, I believe, when the Lord will allow us to be sick in order to teach us to change something in our lifestyle. Sometimes when we have been working very hard, we go down with a bout of 'flu. He wants us to go to bed for a few days so that we can have a really good rest, and have longer to pray with Him! A more extreme example is when the drunkard wakes up the following morning with a splitting headache and feeling sick. The answer is not for him to pray against the sickness and the headache, but for him to resolve to drop the drink.

Sometimes at the end of a long day here, Audrey and I talk over the people we have been praying with. Sometimes we say how lovely it was praying with so-and-so 'because they were so open to receive from the Lord'. At other times we mention sadly that someone 'didn't seem able to receive'. Many things can make it difficult for a person to receive the healing love of Jesus. There may be doubts. Perhaps there is pride. Or maybe, because of past hurts, they just cannot trust Jesus now.

We would never blame people for an inability to receive. It is our role to try to help them to receive the healing power which He is longing to pour out on them. If they are still unable to receive, it is our fault as much as theirs.

But there are those who don't want to receive the healing love of the Lord. A woman came to us who had suffered sickening rejection in her childhood in Ireland, and had been in and out of mental hospital for the past thirty years. We couldn't understand why it was that each time she came to see Audrey and me, she left at peace and with much joy – and yet her husband told us that this only lasted an hour or two. Eventually we asked her, 'Do you want to be healed?' She thought, and then, very sadly, said, 'No'. Being healed would have meant that she would no longer have had everyone round her waiting on her. Instead she would have had to face the responsibility of making something herself of her own life. She wasn't prepared to accept the challenge.

We remember that in a similar way Jesus asked the cripple at the Pool of Bethesda, 'Do you want to get well?' (Jn 5.6).

Sometimes I believe that people are not healed

because we ourselves are praying above the level of our faith. Agnes Sanford wrote that if all those who pray so fervently for the redemption of the world would first learn to pray effectively for the healing of the common cold, we would be getting somewhere. We have seen people's eyesight improve after prayer, but I dread being asked to pray for someone who is totally blind as I have not yet seen such a person healed, and I know I lack the faith to pray with power for such healing. I find the same with autistic children or those who are mentally retarded. So far, we have not yet seen answers to prayer in such cases.

Yet through the grace of God, the frontiers are gradually rolled back. For years I dreaded praying for people with multiple sclerosis. Then there was the glorious afternoon in Bournemouth when a woman who had multiple sclerosis had to be helped into her seat in the front row. After we had prayed with her she walked out unaided.

These may be some of the specific reasons for individual people not being healed when they are prayed for. I believe, however, that there are two much wider and more general reasons why the power of the Lord to heal is often impeded.

One of the most misquoted verses in the Bible comes in Exodus, 'I am the Lord Who heals you' (Ex 15.26). But the promise is conditional. The verse reads, 'If you listen carefully to the voice of the Lord your God and do what is right in His eyes, if you pay attention to His demands and keep all His decrees, I will not bring on you any of the diseases I brought on the Egyptians. For I am the Lord who heals you.' How can we claim today that, as a nation, we listen carefully to the voice of God, do what is right in His eyes and pay attention to His commands and His decrees.'

I do not believe God behaves like a bad-tempered schoolmaster and says, 'They are a rotten disobedient lot. I'm going to pay them out. I'm going to hold back their healing.' I'm sure that it is invariably in His nature to want to heal and to make whole. It is, however, as we follow our own wayward paths and turn away from the Lord and His decrees that we actually cut ourselves off from His healing love. It is not He who deprives us of the healing He longs to give us; it is we who cut ourselves off from being able to receive it.

Then there was the situation in Nazareth. We read that 'Jesus could there do no mighty work . . . and He marvelled because of their unbelief' (Mk 6.5,6, AV). Today we live in a Nazareth-type situation; a spiritual atmosphere which is largely devoid of any real faith in God.

Again, it is not a matter of His saying petulantly, 'I won't heal them, then!' Rather, it is a case of the Lord being saddened by our almost wilful refusal, as a nation, to accept His love and His healing.

But the question which comes naturally to us is: 'Can it be right for us, as individuals who seek to love the Lord and to serve Him, to suffer as a result of the sins of the many?' Yet, in asking that question, we forget that God has made us members of one another. It is obvious that in our daily lives, we are affected, for good or ill, by those around us. All of creation was made as a unity by the same God. Similarly, in spiritual matters, we are affected by the beliefs or unbeliefs of those around us.

There are many reasons why the prayer for healing may not be immediately answered in the way we would like to see. What we must never do, however, is to doubt the nature of God. As Kenneth Hagin says, there is no sickness in heaven. Likewise there is no sickness in God. He is a God of perfect love and it must always be His perfect nature to set free, to comfort, to heal and to make whole.

A missioner once conducted a healing mission in South Africa. He realised that there were more healings among the Africans he prayed for than among the white people. The white people had been taught to believe that God does not heal today. The black people simply accepted that God is a God of love who loves to comfort and to make whole. They had the greater faith.

I believe God always wants to heal, in the sense of making whole and perfect, unless, that is, He wants to give us something even better: for the Christian that may indeed be death, the perfect healing.

But there is one caveat. A theme which runs right through the Bible is this: if you want my help you must follow my way. Jesus said that the most important thing in life is for us to love the Lord our God – with whom Jesus completely identified himself – with all our heart, with all our soul, with all our mind and with all our strength.

Appendix
When People come for Prayer

'The London Healing Mission is the only place I know where you go in as one person and come out another person!' A young man in his early thirties made that remark after his second visit here. Time and again people leave here looking free and happy, and so different from when they came in.

Every day we hear from people who have either telephoned or come here for prayer. They want to give thanks for the way the Lord has answered. Every week at our healing services we read out some of these thanksgivings. Every month we reprint a small selection with my news-letter.

There must be readers who are asking what actually happens when people come here for prayer. To answer that question, I record below thanksgivings from the last five news-letters. They give a better picture of our ministry than if I were to pick out some of the more dramatic healings over a longer period.

However there are those who don't get round to writing to us. I was having lunch with a Christian bookseller, who told me that he had sent two homosexual men to the mission during the previous few months and that both of them had been forgiven, healed, and set free from their homosexuality. I don't think we would ever have known, had the conversation at lunch not turned to the healing of homosexuals.

It would be good if everyone gave thanks to the Lord when He answered prayers. We remember Jesus' experience when only one leper out of the ten who were healed came back to thank Him (Lk 17.12). We reflect that perhaps nine people are blessed here for every one who actually writes or rings to give thanks to the Lord for what He has done for them!

Twice in the last six years I have had a letter from someone questioning whether a particular healing really did take place. In reply we make it clear that we have only the person's word to go on. This is why, wherever possible, we quote verbatim. We are far too busy to check up on individual cases. Nor is it our business. For practical purposes, we rely on what the person tells us that the Lord has done.

As you read through the following thanksgivings, you will see how the Lord has healed in every area; body, mind, soul, and spirit.

C (who has been anorexic) wrote: 'I am pleased to tell you that since my appointment with two members of the team, I have been quite a lot better. I no longer feel the desire to abuse food or take laxatives – in fact the thought of doing so is totally abhorrent to me now. This is quite amazing to me. I always felt that if I ever managed to cease this behaviour it would be due to tremendous effort and will-power on my part, but now I find that the desire has deserted me almost entirely. I still have a long road ahead of me, but I *know* that I shall succeed now, and I praise God for His tremendous mercy and love.'

L: A Christian friend prayed for her hair to grow again (which the doctor said would never happen), and it has! Praise the Lord.

J gave thanks that her back was healed after prayer here.

R wrote: 'The Lord has been doing a mighty work in me, healing memories that go back to the age of four. I am blooming like a rose, just as you prayed for me! Thank you for praying for me. Without these prayers I would never have been healed or saved. Now I am entirely dependent on Him for everything.

J's vicar wrote: 'Can I start by thanking you for the help you have given J and her husband. They went to London apprehensive, and they came home *glowing*. Praise the Lord!'

D told us: 'I asked the mission to pray for my baby, C, as the tear duct in one eye hadn't worked since she was born and she had had many eye infections. Within a month of my prayer request, the tear duct began to function normally and there have been no more infections. Thank you for the Intercessors' prayers, and thank you Jesus for Your wonderful healing.'

B received prayer for fibrositis of the ankles and feet. A month later she told us that about an hour after being prayed for the pain went, and had not returned under any conditions.

M: 'I started writing to you a few days ago to thank you for seeing me, and to say that since then I had suffered a few more attacks of bulima. I got as far as saying "thank you for seeing me", and then suddenly started writing down my feelings, beginning with '*I do not suffer from bulima*'! As I write that I *know* I am cured!'

S, a small boy in hospital with suspected encephalitis. Was prayed for a month ago. Now home and fully recovered.

R told us: 'Four weeks ago you prayed over me for healing of migraine that I'd been having for more than ten years, and praise the Lord with me, that very day I was completely healed!'

M writes: 'My husband was an alcoholic, and finally things became so difficult that we separated. You prayed for me and my marriage situation when you were ministering near my home, and subsequently I came to see you at the mission when I was very depressed. Briefly, I did not find it easy to obey the Lord, but, in doing so in faith, my wildest dreams are now being realised. My husband came to know the Lord in February after I moved back in with him.

'My husband is growing in the love of the Lord and giving open testimonies on Sunday evenings on the seafront. One of our favourite choruses now is "Nothing is too difficult for Thee".'

J wrote: 'I want to thank you for the appointment you gave me, with talk, prayer, and healing prayer as well. It was the most unforgettable day of my life, I shall never forget it. I feel a lot better in body and mind.'

D's wife rang to say he was in deep depression and to ask for prayer. Three days later he was back at work – and five days later was going round the house whistling!

S a friend telephoned recently because she had not long to live with cancer. The doctors are now flabbergasted because the cancer has died instead of her; and although the healing is not quite finished in her bloodstream, the tumour itself has died.

B (a coloured boy in his 'teens) had committed a fairly serious crime and was due for quite a long sentence. He now writes: 'We were on our way to the final hearing in the court when a letter came. My brother opened it and said that the prosecution had dropped the case through lack of evidence. The only reason I can think of why this happened is all the prayers you and all the other people said for me and also the prayers I said myself every time I had a moment. Every time I prayed, I asked God to take the case into His own hands as you told me to, and He listened and He forgave me.'

H wrote: 'I was very grateful to know that all these wonderful people were praying for my parents. I sensed a wonderful feeling of peace. I'm writing now to tell you that my father is improving a lot. He has been told he has no cancer and there is now nothing to worry about. I cannot believe what has happened to my mother – after all these years of hopelessness the pain has gradually receded. As of today, she has had three days without any pain at all. The doctor was puzzled. I told her about your prayers for her and I can't thank you all enough for what you have done.' (We replied saying that it was Jesus who had done it.)

C wrote (from Holland after a ministry weekend there by two of the team): 'I thank the Lord for healing me on the seminar day. I had had blood pressure for a long time and always my hope was that God would heal me. Several times servants of God prayed for me but I was not healed – but that didn't put off my faith – I knew there would be the right day and, at last the day was 24th October. Praise the Lord! I am now free and happy.'

J writes: 'It is with great joy that I can tell you that the bone scan last week revealed that some of the cancer was healed and gone away completely, there are no new spots, and I have finished with chemotherapy. Praise the Lord.

I had such an experience when you prayed with me. It is surely a miracle, when you think that I could hardly walk in July, and the outlook was bleak. Now I have been saved both physically and spiritually.'

M was prayed for by one of the team. She had had a pain in her neck for fifty years now. Immediately after prayer she was able to respond that it was '*already* very much better.'

A wrote: 'The Lord graciously healed me of glaucoma the day after being prayed for at the Mission – May 22nd. I then returned to the specialist who confirmed that the pressure on my eyes was absolutely normal and, thank God, I found my sight was back to normal too. I have thanked the Lord and praised Him ever since and I have never used any more eye drops.

J's wife wrote: 'The pain has not returned since it finally left him last February following our visit to you in January and we thank the Lord for this.'

A wrote: 'Thank you once again for your prayers for Baby D. and Baby S. both fully recovered after both being given the prognosis of "no hope". May God be praised.'

L wrote: 'Having prayed with you on the 30th July this year, I would like to report that on the next occasion I tried to speak in tongues, the language just poured from me. I do not remember having experienced such joy before. It is a tremendous thrill to receive a gift from God and I wish to thank you for your prayers on my behalf.'

R's mother wrote after he had been here for ministry: 'I am absolutely thrilled with R. He is a new man and full of love for the Lord.'

S (15) After prayer his ganglion totally disappeared.

C reminded us that we had prayed for her husband in Durham a few months ago. He had been ill for about sixteen years with a change of personality. He was absolutely right within the week.

L an American woman, was suffering from fear. After one of the team prayed for her, she turned to him and said: 'I just felt the fear go. It's gone!'

J came to see us: As we prayed for him he was sweating from 'flu. He was feeling sick and had a headache. We cut him free from the 'flu in the name of Jesus. He felt very sleepy and half an hour later it had completely gone. No more sweating, no more nausea, no more headache – and he left praising Jesus.

M praises the Lord that He has taken away all desire for cigarettes. She had been a smoker for 27 years and was unable to give up. She asked the Lord to take away the desire as she felt so guilty. One day she suffered a whole day of stomach cramps for no apparent reason and she hasn't smoked since!

L was involved in a road accident. Suffered damage to her coccyx (end of the spine) and had been in pain for a number of months. She was prayed for at the altar rail at one of our Thursday evening services and the pain completely went.

M wrote after one of the team prayed with him: 'Words cannot express my gratitude to you in helping to restore my faith in Almighty God and Jesus Christ His only begotten Son. All frustration and torment were taken away from me during our prayer; and I am left feeling completely at peace and full of joy and confidence for the future.'

G had Hodgkins' disease (can be incurable). He was prayed for at the mission and we have now been told that he has been healed.

B Her hearing has been healed, having been bad since birth. Doctors had said it could never be improved.

A baby of three months which has cried night and day since birth, was prayed for at the mission. We subsequently heard that he immediately ceased crying for two hours, and did not cry at all during the night.

J told us: Through prayer, Paul has been completely healed from Reiter's disease, and is now able to walk again and is back at work.

M came to give thanks that when one of the team prayed for her arthritis a month ago it was completely healed.

A came in to give thanks for the way the Lord had answered prayer when he brought his cousin R to us nearly a year ago with secondary cancer breaking out all over his body. He said that that night (and subsequently too) he slept soundly, which he hadn't done for months. He said that the same evening he threw away all his morphine and cut his pain-killers by half. He lived happily and at peace for much longer than the doctors had believed possible, then died, still happy and at peace. A. came to give thanks for answered prayer.

Miss H wrote: 'Thank you for praying for me and all the sicknesses I had. Jesus healed me.'

S wrote after ministry here: 'I really felt enfolded by Jesus. I know He is walking beside us both, holding our hands. I keep thanking Him for loving me and I know, with His strength, I will pull through.'

J wrote: 'I thought that you would like to know that in 1981 one of the team prayed for me – and God healed me from multiple sclerosis. I have never had any recurrence and God has taken me from a housebound housewife to be a minister's wife in a busy church. God is good, isn't He!'

I: During the time of ministry at a recent teaching day at the mission, she was completely healed of the back pain she had experienced for over thirty years.

M wrote: 'I had an accident in 1950, after which I couldn't see, and was blind for nearly two years. My mother told me to go to Dawson Place, and that was the channel through which God healed me completely.

L In the chapel, one of the team was given a word of knowledge that there was somebody with a pain down the right side of the neck, which the Lord wanted to heal. L. came forward. She had had such a pain for nine months and it had got progressively worse. We prayed for her, and she was healed. She was now able to look right round over her right shoulder without any discomfort at all. How she praised the Lord!

J's back had been covered with spots for seven years. One of the team prayed with her a couple of months ago, and she gave thanks that the back had completely healed up. (All that remain now are a few spots on her neck.)

M came to us feeling knotted up in the base of her tummy, resulting from years of being rejected and abused. After prayer she said that the Lord had healed her and she felt completely free.

Some of these people had been prayed for at one of our healing services. We have these services every

Thursday morning and Thursday evening. I wish we didn't have to call them 'Healing services'. I would rather call them 'Times of worship, at which people get healed.' During the services, we try and put all the emphasis on worshipping the Lord. For it is as we open up our hearts to Him in love and in worship that His healing power comes upon us.

Others had made an appointment with one of the team here, and therefore had one-and-a-half hours to talk through their problems and to pray with the team member. Others had merely telephoned asking for prayer, either for themselves or for a friend. We have four telephone lines and there are always two or three people here every weekday morning and afternoon who are waiting to counsel people and to pray with them over the telephone.

We receive many, many requests for prayer. The number varies from day to day, but it is seldom that we have fewer than ten, and we may receive up to fifty. Invariably those of the team who are here the following day pray through all the previous day's intercessions. We then send out each name (Christian name only) with a brief description of the prayer request, to half a dozen or so of our intercessors. Each intercessor then prays for that person every day for the following month. Thus, when people ring up here for prayer, we ensure that they are well 'soaked' in prayer!

Our intercessors number well over seven hundred and they are spread all over the country, and indeed some are abroad. We shall never know how much we owe them but we know that their prayer support is beyond value. Indeed, recently, the vicar's wife at a large and well-known London church, was heard to say, 'But of course they see miracles at the London

Healing Mission. What do you expect when they have over seven hundred people praying for them every day!'

When Audrey and I came here five years ago, we had virtually no experience of the healing ministry. We came here in obedience to the Lord. He had made it quite clear to us through prayer and through the confirmation of Christian friends that this was where He wanted us to be for the next period of our lives.

When we started work here we kept reminding ourselves that God must have common sense. If He was going to do something so apparently silly as putting a former businessman and a housewife to run a healing mission, then it must follow that He would guide us and show us what to do.

That is what has happened. All the way through the last six years we have had no option but to lean on Him and say in prayer, 'Lord, we don't know what to do. It's up to you. You will have to show us.'

How faithful the Lord has been. We are well aware that we are still learning. We know that we shall still be learning on the day we leave here. But we continue to praise Him for His faithfulness, and more and more we want just to live to His glory and for the spreading of His Kingdom.

Other Highland Books

PRAYERS FOR
HEALING

by

John Gunstone

Prayers for home and hospital; Personal prayers; Corporate prayers; Prayers with responses; Thanksgivings; Praying the Psalms; Praying with the Scriptures; Ministry of reconciliation; Sacramental ministry; A service of prayer for healing; Guide to spontaneous prayer.

A practical and pastoral handbook

LORD HEAL ME

A personal prayer companion

by

John Gunstone

Prayers of compassion, understanding
and faith for personal use

Here are prayers for every kind of illness and
disablement, for emotional disorders as well
as organic ailments. Simple morning and
evening devotions for a patient, plus a selection of prayers for healing by Christians past
and present.

**A fitting gift for a friend who is ill at home
or in hospital**

CANON JOHN GUNSTONE is chairman of
Anglican Renewal Ministries and author of
the highly commended *Prayers for Healing*
now used in many churches.